OXFORD STUD

Series Editor: S

Wilfred Owen:

Selected Poems and Letters

Wilfred Owen

Selected Poems and letters

Wilfred Owen

Selected Poems and Letters

Edited by Helen Cross

Oxford University Press

OXFORD

UNIVERSITY PRESS

Great Clarendon Street, Oxford OX2 6DP

Oxford University Press is a department of the University of Oxford.
It furthers the University's objective of excellence in research, scholarship,
and education by publishing worldwide in

Oxford   New York

Auckland   Cape Town   Dar es Salaam   Hong Kong   Karachi
Kuala Lumpur   Madrid   Melbourne   Mexico City   Nairobi
New Delhi   Shanghai   Taipei   Toronto

With offices in

Argentina   Austria   Brazil   Chile   Czech Republic   France   Greece
Guatemala   Hungary   Italy   Japan   Poland   Portugal   Singapore
South Korea   Switzerland   Thailand   Turkey   Ukraine   Vietnam

Oxford is a registered trade mark of Oxford University Press
in the UK and in certain other countries

British Library Cataloguing in Publication Data

Data available

ISBN: 978-0-19-832878-0

5 7 9 10 8 6

Typeset in India by TNQ

Printed by Printplus, China

Paper used in the production of this book is a natural, recyclable product made from
wood grown in sustainable forests. The manufacturing process conforms to the
environmental regulations of the country of origin.

The publishers would like to thank the following for permission to reproduce photographs:

p2: Oxford University Library; p5: Imperial War Museum; p8: Oxford University Library;
p12: Imperial War Musuem; p16: British Library; p17: Imperial War Musuem;
p112: Corbis/Hulton-Deutsch Collection; p125: Oxford University Library;
p129: Corbis Hulton-Deutsch Collection

Contents

Acknowledgements

The Preface and text of the poems are taken from *Complete Poems and Fragments* edited by Jon Stallworthy (OUP/Chatto & Windus 1983). *Sonnet (Written at Teignmouth, on a Pilgrimage to Keats's House)*, *Nocturne*, *Maundy Thursday*, *On My Songs*, *Soldier's Dream*, and lines from *Supposed Confessions of a Secondrate Sensitive Mind in Dejection*, reprinted by permission of The Random House Group Ltd.

The text of the letters is taken from *Collected Letters* edited by Harold Owen & John Bell (OUP, 1967), reprinted by permission of Oxford University Press.

Laurence Binyon: extract from *For the Fallen* from *Collected Poems* (Macmillan, 1931), reprinted by permission of The Society of Authors as the Literary Representative of the Estate of Laurence Binyon.

John Middleton Murry: extracts from *Evolution of an Intellectual* (Cape, 1927) and from *Aspects of Literature* (Collins, 1921), reprinted by permission of The Society of Authors as the Literary Representative of the Estate of John Middleton Murry.

Siegfried Sassoon: *They* and extracts from *The Death Bed* from *The War Poems* (Faber, 1983); extracts from *The Complete Memoirs of George Sherston* (Faber, 1937), from *Siegfried's Journey 1916–1920* (Faber, 1945), and from his introduction to *Poems by Wilfred Owen* (Chatto & Windus, 1920), all copyright © Siegfried Sassoon, reprinted by permission of the Estate of George Sassoon, c/o Barbara Levy Literary Agency.

W.B. Yeats: extract from *Letters on Poetry from W.B. Yeats to Dorothy Wellesley* (OUP, 1946), reprinted by permission of Oxford University Press.

We have tried to trace and contact all copyright holders before publication. If notified, we will be pleased to rectify any errors or omissions at the earliest opportunity.

Acknowledgements from Helen Cross

I would like to thank Jan Doorly for her patient support throughout this project and for her thoughtful editing. Thank you also to Kate Clements for her help in the final stages and to Steven Croft for his encouragement over the years.

Editors

Steven Croft, the series editor, holds degrees from Leeds and Sheffield universities. He has taught at secondary and tertiary level and headed the Department of English and Humanities in a tertiary college. He has 25 years' examining experience at A level and is currently a Principal Examiner for English. He has written several books on teaching English at A level, and his publications for Oxford University Press include *Exploring Literature, Success in AQA Language and Literature and Exploring Language and Literature*.

Helen Cross read English Literature and Music at the University of Glasgow and later was awarded an MA in Life Writing (with distinction) at the University of York. Over the last twenty years she has taught English and English Literature in comprehensive schools and in the private sector. She is an Associate Lecturer for the Open University and an examiner in A level English Literature. With Steven Croft, she is joint author of A level English Literature textbooks published by Oxford University Press: *Literature, Criticism and Style; Success in Literature; Exploring Literature*.

Foreword

Oxford Student Texts, under the founding editorship of Victor Lee, have established a reputation for presenting literary texts to students in both a scholarly and an accessible way. The new editions aim to build on this successful approach. They have been written to help students, particularly those studying English literature for AS or A level, to develop an increased understanding of their texts. Each volume in the series, which covers a selection of key poetry and drama texts, consists of four main sections which link together to provide an integrated approach to the study of the text.

The first part provides important background information about the writer, his or her times and the factors that played an important part in shaping the work. This discussion sets the work in context and explores some key contextual factors.

This section is followed by the poetry or play itself. The text is presented without accompanying notes so that students can engage with it on their own terms without the influence of secondary ideas. To encourage this approach, the Notes are placed in the third section, immediately following the text. The Notes provide explanations of particular words, phrases, images, allusions and so forth, to help students gain a full understanding of the text. They also raise questions or highlight particular issues or ideas which are important to consider when arriving at interpretations.

The fourth section, Interpretations, goes on to discuss a range of issues in more detail. This involves an examination of the influence of contextual factors as well as looking at such aspects as language and style, and various critical views or interpretations. A range of activities for students to carry out, together with discussions as to how these might be approached, are integrated into this section.

At the end of each volume there is a selection of Essay Questions, a Further Reading list and, where appropriate, a Glossary.

We hope you enjoy reading this text and working with these supporting materials, and wish you every success in your studies.

Steven Croft   *Series Editor*

Wilfred Owen in Context

The war was a terrible and unique experience in the history of mankind; its poetry had likewise to be unique and terrible; it had to record not the high hopes that animated English youth at the outset, but the slow destruction of that youth in the sequel; more than this, it had to record not what the war did to men's bodies and senses, but what it did to their souls. Owen's poetry is unique and terrible because it records imperishably the devastation and the victory of a soul.

(John Middleton Murry, quoted in Hibberd, *Poetry of the First World War*, page 64)

The 'Great War' of 1914–1918 has a remarkable power to stir the imagination. When people think of war, even now, almost a century later, it is very often the First World War that springs to mind. Overriding more recent images of war, the stark wastelands of mud and shattered trees, tin-hatted soldiers, barbed wire and poppies of the First World War have become archetypes of war and remain so even for those born many decades later.

And if the First World War has this particular significance in relation to war, when we think of the poetry of war the name that is most likely to come to mind first is that of Wilfred Owen.

Owen's work has acquired a special meaning for many people. For some, he is *the* representative war poet of all time. He has the mystique of the young soldier-genius, who did not live to fulfil his potential, but was killed, with poignant irony, only a few days before the war ended. Particularly since the 1960s, his angry, moving words have become well known, confronting us with the horror and the pity of war.

Wilfred Owen in 1916

The First World War

The First World War is sometimes described as a journey from innocence to experience. At the beginning of the twentieth century, in the years leading up to the war, many people held a simpler view of life and history than we do today. This was underpinned by the belief that human civilization was perpetually advancing and that progress was always in the direction of what was finer or greater. Traditional moral values seemed safe and reliable; unquestioning faith in religion and in political leaders was much more common; the hierarchical British social-class system was firmly entrenched and conventional gender roles had hardly been challenged. All of these aspects of society were to be thrown into disarray by a war that was shockingly different from anything that had been known before.

The war was sparked when Archduke Franz Ferdinand, heir to the throne of Austro-Hungary, was murdered by a Serbian patriot. This relatively insignificant incident ignited long-standing tensions over territory and fears of German expansionism. Before long most of Europe was involved as a result of a system of treaties that required nations to support their allies. Russia supported Serbia, France had a treaty with Russia, and Britain had one with France. These became known as the 'Allied Powers'. Germany supported Austria, and they were joined by Turkey, to form the 'Central Powers'.

It was by far the most enormous armed conflict that had ever taken place and truly a world war. The fighting extended to Russia, Africa, Turkey, Palestine and the Persian Gulf, as well as to the Atlantic and Pacific oceans, and in 1917 America entered the fray. The number of casualties was staggering: more than 37 million people were killed or wounded.

At the same time, the war was conducted in ways that had been previously unknown. In the past, wars had usually been fought by professional armies, who engaged in battles at a distance from civilian life, but now there was 'total war'. All eligible males were initially encouraged and later conscripted to fight, while all the resources of each nation were focused on the war effort. Advances in technology also changed the face of warfare. Machine guns, tanks, poison gas and new and deadly types of bombs and shells were all used for the first time. At the beginning of the war, soldiers were still trained to fight face-to-face, with bayonets, but this kind of individual combat was soon superseded. Mechanized weapons, which killed impersonally and indiscriminately, became the order of the day.

Another unique feature of the First World War was the notorious trench system. Along the battlefronts each army dug deep ditches, which were lined with sandbags and duckboards and protected by parapets. At intervals there were 'dugouts', or deeper holes, in which men lived, sometimes for months at a time. This system was meant to protect soldiers and equipment, and provide a base from which they could launch attacks. However, bad weather and shelling often reduced much of the trench system to a rat-infested swamp, littered with the festering remains of thousands of corpses. The trench system made possible a 'war of attrition' in which each side tried to wear down the other, and fighting dragged on in what sometimes seemed an interminable stalemate.

Innocence

When Britain joined the conflict in August 1914, people were filled with a patriotic fervour and idealism which, with hindsight, seems painfully naive and out of tune with the real reasons for the war. It was a hundred years since Britain had been directly involved in a major war and no one had any real experience of what war was like. According to A.J.P. Taylor in *The First World War*, 'All imagined that it would be an affair of great marches and great battles, quickly decided' (page 158).

Young men, susceptible to propaganda that presented the war in old-fashioned terms as a moral battle against an evil power,

First World War recruiting poster

signed up willingly. Dying for their country was regarded as an honour, or a religious duty, that would win them 'glory'. Rupert Brooke captured the mood in his sequence of sonnets, *1914*:

> **Now, God be thanked Who has matched us with His hour,**
> **... And caught our youth, and wakened us from sleeping,**
> **With hand made sure, clear eye, and sharpened power**

Recruiting campaigns offered them the opportunity to prove their 'sporting spirit' and earn the respect of future generations.

Wilfred Owen would later lambast this kind of thinking in his famous poem *Dulce et Decorum Est* (page 28). At the time, however, the future war poet was enjoying life in the south of France, well away from all the frantic recruiting and patriotic excitement of England. Poetry was very much on his mind, but not yet war.

Wilfred Owen

The young Wilfred Owen had set his heart on becoming a poet long before war broke out, and he had begun preparing himself for his vocation at a young age.

He was born in 1893 in Oswestry, Shropshire, near the border between England and Wales, and spent the first four years of his life at Plas Wilmot, a substantial villa which had been the home of his mother's family for three generations. When his mother, Susan Shaw, married Tom Owen, a railway clerk, her family was living a lifestyle they couldn't afford, and when her father died, the house had to be sold to pay his debts. From then on, though they were not in dire poverty, the family was never well off. They moved to much smaller premises in Shrewsbury and Birkenhead – a drop in status that Susan, particularly, found humiliating.

Wilfred had three younger siblings: Mary, born in 1895, Harold, in 1897, and Colin, in 1900. In his memoir *Journey from*

Obscurity, Harold suggests that Wilfred, who often took care of the others, was 'denied, if not his boyhood, then his boyishness' and developed a 'quiet gravity' that made him seem older than his years (page 18). Conscious of the need for a good education in order to make his way in the world, Wilfred took his studies very seriously and did well at school, particularly in languages, but he was also fascinated by science and the natural world.

In 1907, at the age of 14, he became a probationer at the Pupil-Teacher Centre at Shrewsbury Technical School. This meant an exhausting combination of studying and teaching in a local school, but was probably the only way he could afford secondary school education. By the time he was finished he was quite sure he did not want to become an elementary school teacher, but the other possibilities – journalism or the civil service – did not appeal to him either. Wilfred wanted to write – and he wanted to write poetry, like Keats. He had discovered the work of the Romantic poets and developed a passionate sense of kinship with Keats. (See Interpretations, page 122).

We can learn a great deal about Owen and his thoughts and feelings from reading his letters. He had an unusually close relationship with his mother and throughout his short life wrote to her every few days when he was away from home. He shared with her a great deal about his hopes, disappointments and ambitions. Ideally, he would have liked to study full time at a university – Oxford, perhaps – but it was out of the question for financial reasons. The only way he could continue his education was to find some way to support himself which would allow him to study, in his spare time, as an external student.

He had been deeply religious as a boy, influenced by his mother, who hoped he might become a priest. An opportunity to serve as assistant to the vicar of Dunsden, a country parish in Oxfordshire, offered a way forward for a time, but ended disastrously. He all but lost his religious faith and was forced to return home, close to breakdown. (See Interpretations, page 118.)

Owen joined the Artists' Rifles in 1915; this picture shows
the group in November of that year

In September 1913 he left England and travelled to Bordeaux
to teach English at the Berlitz language school. Though the work
was very demanding he found the change of lifestyle refreshing.
Then, in the summer of 1914, he was invited to spend the
summer at a villa in the Pyrenees, as private tutor to a Parisian
family. News of the war rumbled on, but it was not often in the
foreground of Owen's mind. He had just been introduced to the
French poet and philosopher Laurent Tailhade, who was to
become an influential mentor and friend. (See Interpretations,
page 124.) So while the young men of England were responding
to recruiting propaganda and idealistically queuing to enlist in
the army, Owen was happier than he had been for a long time,
enjoying himself amid beautiful scenery and absorbing new ideas
about poetry, philosophy and life.

'The war affects me less than it ought. But I can do no service to anybody by agitating for news or making dole over the slaughter', Owen wrote in August 1914. He remained in France for another year, working as a freelance English teacher and experimenting with poetry, enjoying his independence, but still agonizing about career possibilities and his potential as a writer. (See Letter 330, 5 March 1915, on page 51.) Influenced by Tailhade, Owen felt he would have more value as a living poet than a dead soldier, though he did think it might be worth fighting to preserve 'the language in which Keats and the rest of them wrote'. Otherwise, though he had moments of guilt, he did not feel particularly patriotic: 'I do not know in what else England is greatly superior, or dearer to me, than another land and people' (Letter 302, 2 December 1914, John Bell: *Selected Letters* [SL] page 130).

A short visit to London the following summer changed his mind and he decided to join the 'Artists' Rifles'. He told his mother: 'I don't want the bore of training, I don't want to wear khaki; nor yet to save my honour before inquisitive grand-children fifty years hence. But I <u>now</u> <u>do</u> most <u>intensely</u> <u>want</u> <u>to</u> <u>fight</u>' (Letter 357, 20 June 1915, SL, page 153).

He entered the army in October 1915, just before the government introduced compulsory conscription. After six months' training, he was commissioned as a second lieutenant in the 5th Battalion of the Manchester Regiment, stationed in Surrey and then Lancashire. He was in charge of a platoon of about 40 men of all ages, of whom some were far more experienced than he was. To maintain his authority as an officer, he was expected to prove his expertise and distance himself from the lower ranks. The army had strict class distinctions: officers were drawn from the better-educated middle classes, whereas the majority of ordinary soldiers were working-class 'Tommies'. Initially, it sounds as if Owen felt like a fish out of water: 'I am marooned on a Crag of Superiority in an ocean of Soldiers' (Letter 439, 19 June 1916, SL, page 188).

During 1916, army discipline left him little opportunity to write, although he did manage to find time to visit The Poetry Bookshop in London, a venture started by Harold Monro, whose aim was to encourage reading and discussion of poetry and nurture talented writers. Monro, along with the classical scholar and translator Edward Marsh, published *Georgian Poetry* – a series of anthologies in what was then considered a more modern style. He was impressed by Owen's work, but encouraged him to be a little less Romantic and more modern.

Owen's letters from 1916 are full of the details of army life and training, but say almost nothing about the war itself. He doesn't seem at that stage to have had any doubts about the conventional view of soldiering – that 'preparing... to lay down our lives for another, [was] the highest moral act possible' (Letter 425, 18 March 1916, *SL*, page 184). Soldiers were not supposed to discuss the war: 'It was enough to be sure that Germany was bad and victory certain' (Dominic Hibberd, *Wilfred Owen*, page 212). Yet he must have seen the long casualty lists and been aware that news from France was not good.

Eventually, in December 1916, he received his first overseas posting. On 1 January 1917, he wrote: 'There is a fine heroic feeling about being in France, and I am in perfect spirits. A tinge of excitement is about me, but excitement is always necessary to my happiness' (Letter 475, 1 January 1917, *SL*, page 207).

Experience

From 1916 onwards, attitudes to the war began to change. The Battle of the Somme, which raged over the summer, marks the turning point. On 1 July, the Allies launched a huge offensive in the area of the River Somme, but planning and preparation were poor and the strength of the German defences had been underestimated. Very little was achieved. There were 60,000 British casualties on the first day alone, and more than a million lives were lost overall. People began to question whether slaughter on this scale was worthwhile. For the remainder of the war, critical and dissenting voices became more and more prominent.

Wilfred Owen's first experience of the trenches was short, but it had a powerful effect on him and dramatically changed his perceptions and outlook. Over a few days in January 1917 he 'suffered seventh hell', as he wrote to his mother. His letters (see pages 54–8) give a vivid impression of his experience: freezing weather, terrible conditions, heavy bombardments and men dying around him. Thoroughly disillusioned, he could now see that dying in war was not at all glorious. Anyone who wrote that it was would have to be either naive or dishonest. Over the next year and a half Owen would draw on these experiences to create some of his greatest war poems.

During March and April 1917 Owen was involved in action near St Quentin, where the Germans had constructed a new trench system known as the 'Hindenburg Line'. He confronted further horrors, and experienced going 'over the top', when lines of men had to advance out of the trenches and across open ground in full view of the enemy. He gave an impression of this later in *Spring Offensive* (page 48; see Notes, page 99). Many men died, including two of Owen's closest friends.

One night soon afterwards Owen was asleep on a railway embankment when a shell exploded right beside him. Although he was not physically injured, he was knocked unconscious. When he came to he found himself lying in a small hole, where he remained for several days. One of his friends had been blown to pieces and his body lay 'in various places round about'. Combined with the strain of the previous few weeks, this brought on 'shell shock' or neurasthenia. Nowadays this would be recognized as Post-Traumatic Stress Disorder, but then it was sometimes dismissed as cowardice or shirking. Men who collapsed under the strain, like the soldier in *The Dead-Beat* (page 29), were often branded malingerers, even by doctors.

British troops go 'over the top'

Owen spent some weeks in a Casualty Clearing Station before he was sent home and then on to Craiglockhart War Hospital for Neurasthenic Officers near Edinburgh. Apart from the stammering and shaking typical of shell shock, his main symptom was terrible nightmares, some of which appear in poems such as *Dulce et Decorum Est* (page 28) and *The Sentry* (page 47). The poet Siegfried Sassoon, who arrived at Craiglockhart a few weeks later, gives an impression of the place in his fictionalized memoir, *Sherston's Progress*:

> By daylight, the doctors dealt successfully with these disadvantages, and [Craiglockhart], so to speak, 'made cheerful conversation'.
>
> But by night they lost control and the hospital became sepulchral and oppressive with saturations of war experience. One lay awake

and listened to feet padding along passages which smelt of stale cigarette-smoke; for the nurses couldn't prevent insomnia-ridden officers from smoking half the night in their bedrooms, though the locks had been removed from all doors. One became conscious that the place was full of men whose slumbers were morbid and terrifying – men muttering uneasily or suddenly crying out in their sleep. Around me was that underworld of dreams haunted by submerged memories of warfare and its intolerable shocks and self-lacerating failures to achieve the impossible.

(Sassoon, *Sherston's Progress*, pages 556–7)

Grim though it was, however, it was a lot less grim than being at the Front. Owen was lucky to be assigned to a doctor who encouraged his patients to pursue their interests, to be active and in contact with nature. Not all army psychiatrists were so progressive. As Owen's condition improved, he was encouraged to work on his poetry. Most fortunate of all, Craiglockhart brought him into contact with Sassoon.

Up to this point, Owen had hardly considered the war as a subject for poetry. In one or two poems he had begun to question war in a general sense, but he still held the conventional view that it was necessary to continue until 'arrogant' Germany had been defeated.

Sassoon had been in the trenches and witnessed the beginning of the offensive on the Somme in July 1916. He was friendly with famous pacifists, including Bertrand Russell, and came to believe that the government could have ended the war by diplomacy but had chosen not to for political reasons, and had thus sacrificed thousands of men unnecessarily. Sassoon had announced this in a famous public statement in which he also criticized the civilian population for their 'callous complacency' and apparent indifference to the suffering of the soldiers. In order to suppress his protest the authorities decided he had suffered a 'nervous breakdown' and sent him to Craiglockhart. There he continued to express his views equally forcefully, but through the safer medium of poetry.

Owen had heard about this and read Sassoon's work and was hugely excited by the possibility of meeting him. He plucked up the courage to introduce himself and show Sassoon some of his work. Sassoon encouraged him to 'Sweat [his] guts out writing poetry,' but admitted later that he did not immediately recognize Owen's talent:

> It was, however, not until some time in October, when he brought me his splendidly constructed sonnet *Anthem for Doomed Youth*, that it dawned on me that my little friend was much more than the promising minor poet I had hitherto adjudged him to be. I now realized that his verse, with its sumptuous epithets and large-scale imagery, its noble naturalness and depth of meaning, had impressive affinities with Keats, whom he took as his supreme exemplar. This new sonnet was a revelation. ... After assuring him of its excellence I told him that I would do my best to get it published in *The Nation*.
>
> (Sassoon, *Siegfried's Journey, 1916–20*, pages 59–60)

With Sassoon's friendship and support Owen grew in confidence. Sassoon helped him to meet influential literary friends and may also have enabled him to feel more comfortable with his sexuality. It has been suggested that both were homosexuals, and homosexuality at that time was against the law and often considered evil by conventional people. Sassoon also introduced Owen to the work of other writers who wrote realistically and critically about the war, and passed on the advice he had been given by Edward Marsh that poetry should be true to experience.

Owen began to write directly about his war experience, becoming openly critical of those in authority, experimenting with sarcasm and colloquial language in the manner of Sassoon, and gradually toning down the Romantic elements of his style. (See Interpretations, page 129.) He had always wanted to be a poet, but there is little doubt that Sassoon gave him the impetus he needed to succeed. A few weeks after their first meeting Owen wrote:

> ... you have <u>fixed</u> my Life – however short. You did not light me: I was always a mad comet; but you have fixed me. I spun round you a satellite for a month, but I shall swing out soon, a dark star in the orbit where you will blaze.
>
> (Letter 557, 5 November 1917, *SL*, page 289)

By the end of 1917 Owen was pronounced fit enough to return to his battalion, now stationed in Yorkshire, for 'light duties', which turned out to mean supervising all the domestic arrangements. In between duties and training Owen would have liked to 'sweat his guts out writing poetry', but only had about three free hours a week. However, he managed to complete about twenty war poems and began planning a book that was to expose 'the pity of war'. His draft Preface for the book is on page 19.

Owen's friends tried to get work for him at the War Office, but nothing came of the plan. Meanwhile, Sassoon had gone back to the Front to be with his men, but he returned injured. By the time Owen received his second posting to France he had come to the conclusion that if his job as a poet was to speak for the soldiers, he had to be there with them. He felt that if his poetry was to be taken seriously, he would need to have earned a reputation for bravery. Otherwise people would dismiss his protest, as some critics later did, as the work of a 'broken man' (see Interpretations, pages 147–8). Owen and Sassoon were well aware that their view of the war was very different from that of wider society. September 1918 found Owen once more exercising troops and feeling like a 'cattle driver'.

Earlier in the year, and after many months of stalemate, the Germans had launched a huge 'Spring Offensive'. This had been halted with the assistance of the Americans, and the Allies were now advancing towards victory. Owen found himself once more involved in attacking the Hindenburg Line and, though casualties

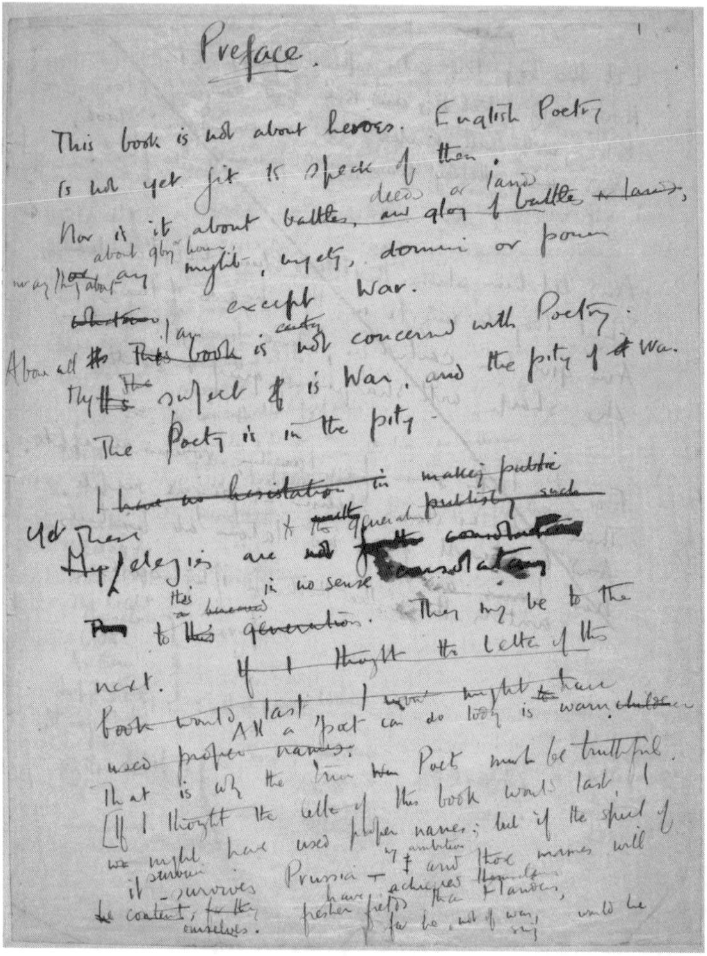

A facsimile of Owen's draft Preface

were high, this time there was a breakthrough. He was awarded the Military Cross for his part in this action. Aware that the war was drawing to a close, Owen began to look forward to a promising future in the London literary scene. Now that his courage had been recognized officially, he would be confident to speak out for the survivors of the war.

It was during a further attack on 4 November, attempting a crossing of the Sambre–Oise Canal, that Wilfred Owen was shot and killed. One week later, the Armistice was declared.

The Sambre–Oise Canal, November 1918

Selected Poems of Wilfred Owen

Preface

This book is not about heroes. English poetry is not yet fit to speak of them.

Nor is it about deeds, or lands, nor anything about glory, honour, might, majesty, dominion, or power, except War.

Above all I am not concerned with Poetry.

My subject is War, and the pity of War.

The Poetry is in the pity.

Yet these elegies are to this generation in no sense consolatory. They may be to the next. All a poet can do today is warn. That is why the true Poets must be truthful.

(If I thought the letter of this book would last, I might have used proper names; but if the spirit of it survives – survives Prussia – my ambition and those names will have achieved themselves fresher fields than Flanders...)

Sonnet

Written at Teignmouth, on a Pilgrimage to Keats's House

Three colours have I known the Deep to wear;
'Tis well today that Purple grandeurs gloom,
Veiling the Emerald sheen and Sky-blue glare.
Well, too, that lowly-brooding clouds now loom
5 In sable majesty around, fringed fair
With ermine-white of surf: to me they bear

Watery memorials of His mystic doom
Whose Name was writ in Water (saith his tomb).

Eternally may sad waves wail his death,
10 Choke in their grief 'mongst rocks where he has lain,
Or heave in silence, yearning with hushed breath,
While mournfully trail the slow-moved mists and rain,
And softly the small drops slide from weeping trees
Quivering in anguish to the sobbing breeze.

Nocturne

Now, as the warm approach of honied slumber blurs
    my sense,
Before I yield me to th'enchantment of my bed,
God rest all souls in toil and turbulence,
All men a-weary seeking bread;
5 God rest them all tonight!
Let sleep expunge
The day's monotonous vistas from their sight;
And let them plunge
Deep down the dusky firmament of reverie
10 And drowse of dreams with me.

Ah! I should drowse away the night most peacefully
But that there toil too many bodies unreposed
Who fain would fall on lethargy;
Too many leaden eyes unclosed;
15 And aching hands amove
Interminably,
Beneath the light that night will not remove;
Too many brains that rave in dust and steam!
They rave, but cannot dream!

Happiness

Ever again to breathe pure happiness,
So happy that we gave away our toy?
We smiled at nothings, needing no caress?
Have we not laughed too often since with Joy?
5   Have we not stolen too strange and sorrowful wrongs
For her hands' pardoning? The sun may cleanse,
And time, and starlight. Life will sing great songs,
And Gods will show us pleasures more than men's.

Yet heaven looks smaller than the old doll's-home,
10 No nestling place is left in bluebell bloom,
And the wide arms of trees have lost their scope.
The former happiness is unreturning:
Boys' griefs are not so grievous as youth's yearning,
Boys have no sadness sadder than our hope.

Inspection

'You! What d'you mean by this?' I rapped.
'You dare come on parade like this?'
'Please, sir, it's –' ''Old yer mouth,' the sergeant snapped.
'I takes 'is name, sir?' – 'Please, and then dismiss.'

5   Some days 'confined to camp' he got,
For being 'dirty on parade'.
He told me, afterwards, the damnèd spot
Was blood, his own. 'Well, blood is dirt,' I said.

'Blood's dirt,' he laughed, looking away,
10 Far off to where his wound had bled
And almost merged for ever into clay.
'The world is washing out its stains,' he said.
'It doesn't like our cheeks so red:
Young blood's its great objection.
15 But when we're duly white-washed, being dead
The race will bear Field Marshal God's inspection.'

Anthem for Doomed Youth

What passing-bells for these who die as cattle?
    – Only the monstrous anger of the guns.
    Only the stuttering rifles' rapid rattle
Can patter out their hasty orisons.
5 No mockeries now for them; no prayers nor bells;
    Nor any voice of mourning save the choirs, –
The shrill, demented choirs of wailing shells;
    And bugles calling for them from sad shires.

What candles may be held to speed them all?
10   Not in the hands of boys but in their eyes
Shall shine the holy glimmers of goodbyes.
    The pallor of girls' brows shall be their pall;
Their flowers the tenderness of patient minds,
And each slow dusk a drawing-down of blinds.

Maundy Thursday

Between the brown hands of a server-lad
The silver cross was offered to be kissed.
The men came up, lugubrious, but not sad,
And knelt reluctantly, half-prejudiced.
5 (And kissing, kissed the emblem of a creed.)
Then mourning women knelt; meek mouths they had,
(And kissed the Body of the Christ indeed.)
Young children came, with eager lips and glad.
(These kissed a silver doll, immensely bright.)
10 Then I, too, knelt before that acolyte.
Above the crucifix, I bent my head:
The Christ was thin, and cold, and very dead:
And yet I bowed, yea, kissed – my lips did cling.
(I kissed the warm live hand that held the thing.)

On My Songs

Though unseen Poets, many and many a time,
Have answered me as if they knew my woe,
And it might seem have fashioned so their rime
To be my own soul's cry; easing the flow
5 Of my dumb tears with language sweet as sobs,
Yet are there days when all these hoards of thought
Hold nothing for me. Not one verse that throbs
Throbs with my heart, or as my brain is fraught.

'Tis then I voice mine own weird reveries:
10 Low croonings of a motherless child, in gloom
Singing his frightened self to sleep, are these.
One night, if thou shouldst lie in this Sick Room,

Dreading the Dark thou darest not illume,
Listen; my voice may haply lend thee ease.

1914

War broke: and now the Winter of the world
With perishing great darkness closes in.
The foul tornado, centred at Berlin,
Is over all the width of Europe whirled,
5   Rending the sails of progress. Rent or furled
Are all Art's ensigns. Verse wails. Now begin
Famines of thought and feeling. Love's wine's thin.
The grain of human Autumn rots, down-hurled.

For after Spring had bloomed in early Greece,
10   And Summer blazed her glory out with Rome,
An Autumn softly fell, a harvest home,
A slow grand age, and rich with all increase.
But now, for us, wild Winter, and the need
Of sowings for new Spring, and blood for seed.

I Saw His Round Mouth's Crimson

I saw his round mouth's crimson deepen as it fell,
    Like a sun, in his last deep hour;
Watched the magnificent recession of farewell,
    Clouding, half gleam, half glower,
5   And a last splendour burn the heavens of his cheek.
    And in his eyes
The cold stars lighting, very old and bleak,
    In different skies.

Apologia pro Poemate Meo

I, too, saw God through mud, –
    The mud that cracked on cheeks when wretches smiled.
    War brought more glory to their eyes than blood,
    And gave their laughs more glee than shakes a child.

5   Merry it was to laugh there –
    Where death becomes absurd and life absurder.
    For power was on us as we slashed bones bare
    Not to feel sickness or remorse of murder.

I, too, have dropped off Fear –
10 Behind the barrage, dead as my platoon,
    And sailed my spirit surging light and clear
    Past the entanglement where hopes lay strewn;

And witnessed exultation –
    Faces that used to curse me, scowl for scowl,
15 Shine and lift up with passion of oblation,
    Seraphic for an hour; though they were foul.

I have made fellowships –
    Untold of happy lovers in old song.
    For love is not the binding of fair lips
20 With the soft silk of eyes that look and long,

By Joy, whose ribbon slips, –
    But wound with war's hard wire whose stakes are strong;
    Bound with the bandage of the arm that drips;
    Knit in the webbing of the rifle-thong.

25 I have perceived much beauty
    In the hoarse oaths that kept our courage straight;

Heard music in the silentness of duty;
Found peace where shell-storms spouted reddest spate.

Nevertheless, except you share
30   With them in hell the sorrowful dark of hell,
Whose world is but the trembling of a flare
And heaven but as the highway for a shell,

You shall not hear their mirth:
You shall not come to think them well content
35   By any jest of mine. These men are worth
Your tears. You are not worth their merriment.

At a Calvary near the Ancre

One ever hangs where shelled roads part.
    In this war He too lost a limb,
But His disciples hide apart;
    And now the Soldiers bear with Him.

5   Near Golgotha strolls many a priest,
    And in their faces there is pride
That they were flesh-marked by the Beast
    By whom the gentle Christ's denied.

The scribes on all the people shove
10   And bawl allegiance to the state,
But they who love the greater love
    Lay down their life; they do not hate.

Miners

There was a whispering in my hearth
  A sigh of the coal,
Grown wistful of a former earth
  It might recall.

5 I listened for a tale of leaves
  And smothered ferns,
Frond-forests, and the low sly lives
  Before the fauns.

My fire might show steam-phantoms simmer
10 From Time's old cauldron,
Before the birds made nests in summer,
  Or men had children.

But the coals were murmuring of their mine,
  And moans down there
15 Of boys that slept wry sleep, and men
  Writhing for air.

And I saw white bones in the cinder-shard,
  Bones without number.
Many the muscled bodies charred,
20 And few remember.

I thought of all that worked dark pits
  Of war, and died
Digging the rock where Death reputes
  Peace lies indeed.

25 Comforted years will sit soft-chaired,
  In rooms of amber;

The years will stretch their hands, well-cheered
  By our life's ember;

The centuries will burn rich loads
30 With which we groaned,
Whose warmth shall lull their dreaming lids,
  While songs are crooned;
But they will not dream of us poor lads,
  Left in the ground.

Dulce et Decorum Est

Bent double, like old beggars under sacks,
Knock-kneed, coughing like hags, we cursed through
 sludge,
Till on the haunting flares we turned our backs
And towards our distant rest began to trudge.
5 Men marched asleep. Many had lost their boots
But limped on, blood-shod. All went lame; all blind;
Drunk with fatigue; deaf even to the hoots
Of tired, outstripped Five-Nines that dropped behind.

Gas! GAS! Quick, boys! – An ecstasy of fumbling,
10 Fitting the clumsy helmets just in time;
But someone still was yelling out and stumbling,
And flound'ring like a man in fire or lime…
Dim, through the misty panes and thick green light,
As under a green sea, I saw him drowning.

15 In all my dreams, before my helpless sight,
He plunges at me, guttering, choking, drowning.

If in some smothering dreams you too could pace
Behind the wagon that we flung him in,
And watch the white eyes writhing in his face,
20   His hanging face, like a devil's sick of sin;
If you could hear, at every jolt, the blood
Come gargling from the froth-corrupted lungs,
Obscene as cancer, bitter as the cud
Of vile, incurable sores on innocent tongues, –
25   My friend, you would not tell with such high zest
To children ardent for some desperate glory
The old Lie: Dulce et decorum est
Pro patria mori.

The Dead-Beat

He dropped, – more sullenly than wearily,
Lay stupid like a cod, heavy like meat,
And none of us could kick him to his feet;
– Just blinked at my revolver, blearily;
5   – Didn't appear to know a war was on,
Or see the blasted trench at which he stared.
'I'll do 'em in,' he whined. 'If this hand's spared,
I'll murder them, I will.'

A low voice said
'It's Blighty, p'raps, he sees; his pluck's all gone,
10   Dreaming of all the valiant, that *aren't* dead:
Bold uncles, smiling ministerially;
Maybe his brave young wife, getting her fun
In some new home, improved materially.
It's not these stiffs have crazed him; nor the Hun.'

15 We sent him down at last, out of the way.
    Unwounded; – stout lad, too, before that strafe.
    Malingering? Stretcher-bearers winked, 'Not half!'

    Next day I heard the Doc's well-whiskied laugh:
    'That scum you sent last night soon died. Hooray!'

Insensibility

1
Happy are men who yet before they are killed
Can let their veins run cold.
Whom no compassion fleers
Or makes their feet
5   Sore on the alleys cobbled with their brothers.
The front line withers.
But they are troops who fade, not flowers,
For poets' tearful fooling:
Men, gaps for filling:
10 Losses, who might have fought
Longer, but no one bothers.

2
And some cease feeling
Even themselves or for themselves.
Dullness best solves
15 The tease and doubt of shelling,
And Chance's strange arithmetic
Comes simpler than the reckoning of their shilling.
They keep no check on armies' decimation.

3

Happy are these who lose imagination:
20   They have enough to carry with ammunition.
Their spirit drags no pack.
Their old wounds, save with cold, can not more ache.
Having seen all things red,
Their eyes are rid
25   Of the hurt of the colour of blood for ever.
And terror's first constriction over,
Their hearts remain small-drawn.
Their senses in some scorching cautery of battle
Now long since ironed,
30   Can laugh among the dying, unconcerned.

4

Happy the soldier home, with not a notion
How somewhere, every dawn, some men attack,
And many sighs are drained.
Happy the lad whose mind was never trained:
35   His days are worth forgetting more than not.
He sings along the march
Which we march taciturn, because of dusk,
The long, forlorn, relentless trend
From larger day to huger night.

5

40   We wise, who with a thought besmirch
Blood over all our soul,
How should we see our task
But through his blunt and lashless eyes?
Alive, he is not vital overmuch;
45   Dying, not mortal overmuch;
Nor sad, nor proud,
Nor curious at all.

He cannot tell
Old men's placidity from his.

6

50 But cursed are dullards whom no cannon stuns,
That they should be as stones.
Wretched are they, and mean
With paucity that never was simplicity.
By choice they made themselves immune
55 To pity and whatever moans in man
Before the last sea and the hapless stars;
Whatever mourns when many leave these shores;
Whatever shares
The eternal reciprocity of tears.

Strange Meeting

It seemed that out of battle I escaped
Down some profound dull tunnel, long since scooped
Through granites which titanic wars had groined.

Yet also there encumbered sleepers groaned,
5 Too fast in thought or death to be bestirred.
Then, as I probed them, one sprang up, and stared
With piteous recognition in fixed eyes,
Lifting distressful hands, as if to bless.
And by his smile, I knew that sullen hall, –
10 By his dead smile I knew we stood in Hell.

With a thousand pains that vision's face was grained;
Yet no blood reached there from the upper ground,
And no guns thumped, or down the flues made moan.

'Strange friend' I said, 'here is no cause to mourn.'
15 'None,' said that other, 'save the undone years,
The hopelessness. Whatever hope is yours,
Was my life also; I went hunting wild
After the wildest beauty in the world,
Which lies not calm in eyes, or braided hair,
20 But mocks the steady running of the hour,
And if it grieves, grieves richlier than here.
For by my glee might many men have laughed,
And of my weeping something had been left,
Which must die now. I mean the truth untold,
25 The pity of war, the pity war distilled.
Now men will go content with what we spoiled,
Or, discontent, boil bloody, and be spilled.
They will be swift with swiftness of the tigress.
None will break ranks, though nations trek from progress.
30 Courage was mine, and I had mystery,
Wisdom was mine, and I had mastery:
To miss the march of this retreating world
Into vain citadels that are not walled.
Then, when much blood had clogged their chariot-wheels,
35 I would go up and wash them from sweet wells,
Even with truths that lie too deep for taint.
I would have poured my spirit without stint
But not through wounds; not on the cess of war.
Foreheads of men have bled where no wounds were.

40 'I am the enemy you killed, my friend.
I knew you in this dark: for so you frowned
Yesterday through me as you jabbed and killed.
I parried; but my hands were loath and cold.
Let us sleep now...'

Arms and the Boy

Let the boy try along this bayonet-blade
How cold steel is, and keen with hunger of blood;
Blue with all malice, like a madman's flash;
And thinly drawn with famishing for flesh.

5 Lend him to stroke these blind, blunt bullet-leads,
Which long to nuzzle in the hearts of lads,
Or give him cartridges whose fine zinc teeth
Are sharp with sharpness of grief and death.

For his teeth seem for laughing round an apple.
10 There lurk no claws behind his fingers supple;
And God will grow no talons at his heels,
Nor antlers through the thickness of his curls.

The Show

We have fallen in the dreams the ever-living
Breathe on the tarnished mirror of the world,
And then smooth out with ivory hands and sigh.

W.B.YEATS

My soul looked down from a vague height, with Death,
As unremembering how I rose or why,
And saw a sad land, weak with sweats of dearth,
Grey, cratered like the moon with hollow woe,
5 And pitted with great pocks and scabs of plagues.

Across its beard, that horror of harsh wire,
There moved thin caterpillars, slowly uncoiled.

It seemed they pushed themselves to be as plugs
Of ditches, where they writhed and shrivelled, killed.

10   By them had slimy paths been trailed and scraped
Round myriad warts that might be little hills.

From gloom's last dregs these long-strewn creatures crept,
And vanished out of dawn down hidden holes.

(And smell came up from those foul openings
15   As out of mouths, or deep wounds deepening.)

On dithering feet upgathered, more and more,
Brown strings, towards strings of grey, with bristling
   spines,
All migrants from green fields, intent on mire.

Those that were grey, of more abundant spawns,
20   Ramped on the rest and ate them and were eaten.

I saw their bitten backs curve, loop, and straighten.
I watched those agonies curl, lift, and flatten.

Whereat, in terror what that sight might mean,
I reeled and shivered earthward like a feather.

25   And Death fell with me, like a deepening moan.
And He, picking a manner of worm, which half
   had hid
Its bruises in the earth, but crawled no further,
Showed me its feet, the feet of many men,
And the fresh-severed head of it, my head.

Futility

Move him into the sun –
Gently its touch awoke him once,
At home, whispering of fields half-sown.
Always it woke him, even in France,
5   Until this morning and this snow.
If anything might rouse him now
The kind old sun will know.

Think how it wakes the seeds –
Woke once the clays of a cold star.
10   Are limbs, so dear achieved, are sides
Full-nerved, still warm, too hard to stir?
Was it for this the clay grew tall?
– O what made fatuous sunbeams toil
To break earth's sleep at all?

Greater Love

Red lips are not so red
    As the stained stones kissed by the English dead.
Kindness of wooed and wooer
Seems shame to their love pure.
5   O Love, your eyes lose lure
    When I behold eyes blinded in my stead!

Your slender attitude
    Trembles not exquisite like limbs knife-skewed,
Rolling and rolling there
10   Where God seems not to care;
Till the fierce love they bear
    Cramps them in death's extreme decrepitude.

Your voice sings not so soft, –
 Though even as wind murmuring through raftered
  loft, –
15 Your dear voice is not dear,
Gentle, and evening clear,
As theirs whom none now hear,
 Now earth has stopped their piteous mouths that
  coughed.

Heart, you were never hot
20 Nor large, nor full like hearts made great with shot;
And though your hand be pale,
Paler are all which trail
Your cross through flame and hail:
 Weep, you may weep, for you may touch them not.

The Last Laugh

'Oh! Jesus Christ! I'm, hit,' he said; and died.
Whether he vainly cursed or prayed indeed,
 The Bullets chirped – In vain, vain, vain!
 Machine-guns chuckled – Tut-tut! Tut-tut!
5 And the Big Gun guffawed.

Another sighed – 'Oh Mother, – Mother, – Dad!'
Then smiled at nothing, childlike, being dead.
 And the lofty Shrapnel-cloud
 Leisurely gestured, – Fool!
10 And the splinters spat, and tittered.

'My Love!' one moaned. Love-languid seemed his mood,
Till slowly lowered, his whole face kissed the mud.
 And the Bayonets' long teeth grinned;

                Rabbles of Shells hooted and groaned;
15   And the Gas hissed.

Mental Cases

Who are these? Why sit they here in twilight?
Wherefore rock they, purgatorial shadows,
Drooping tongues from jaws that slob their relish,
Baring teeth that leer like skulls' teeth wicked?
5   Stroke on stroke of pain, – but what slow panic,
Gouged these chasms round their fretted sockets?
Ever from their hair and through their hands' palms
Misery swelters. Surely we have perished
Sleeping, and walk hell; but who these hellish?

10   – These are men whose minds the Dead have ravished.
Memory fingers in their hair of murders,
Multitudinous murders they once witnessed.
Wading sloughs of flesh these helpless wander,
Treading blood from lungs that had loved laughter.
15   Always they must see these things and hear them,
Batter of guns and shatter of flying muscles,
Carnage incomparable, and human squander
Rucked too thick for these men's extrication.

Therefore still their eyeballs shrink tormented
20   Back into their brains, because on their sense
Sunlight seems a blood-smear; night comes blood-black;
Dawn breaks open like a wound that bleeds afresh.
– Thus their heads wear this hilarious, hideous,
Awful falseness of set-smiling corpses.
25   – Thus their hands are plucking at each other;
Picking at the rope-knouts of their scourging;

Searching after us who smote them, brother,
Pawing us who dealt them war and madness.

The Chances

I 'mind as how the night before that show
Us five got talkin'; we was in the know.
'Ah well,' says Jimmy, and he's seen some scrappin',
'There ain't no more than five things as can happen, –
5   You get knocked out; else wounded, bad or cushy;
Scuppered; or nowt except you're feelin' mushy.'

One of us got the knock-out, blown to chops;
One lad was hurt, like, losin' both his props;
And one – to use the word of hypocrites –
10   Had the misfortune to be took by Fritz.
Now me, I wasn't scratched, praise God Almighty,
Though next time, please, I'll thank Him for a blighty.
But poor old Jim, he's livin' and he's not;
He reckoned he'd five chances, and he had:
15   He's wounded, killed, and pris'ner, all the lot,
The flamin' lot all rolled in one. Jim's mad.

The Send-Off

Down the close darkening lanes they sang their way
To the siding-shed,
And lined the train with faces grimly gay.

Their breasts were stuck all white with wreath and spray
5   As men's are, dead.

39

Dull porters watched them, and a casual tramp
Stood staring hard,
Sorry to miss them from the upland camp.

Then, unmoved, signals nodded, and a lamp
10   Winked to the guard.

So secretly, like wrongs hushed-up, they went.
They were not ours:
We never heard to which front these were sent;

Nor there if they yet mock what women meant
15   Who gave them flowers.

Shall they return to beating of great bells
In wild train-loads?
A few, a few, too few for drums and yells,

May creep back, silent, to village wells
20   Up half-known roads.

The Parable of the Old Man and the Young

So Abram rose, and clave the wood, and went,
And took the fire with him, and a knife.
And as they sojourned both of them together,
Isaac the first-born spake and said, My Father,
5   Behold the preparations, fire and iron,
But where the lamb, for this burnt-offering?
Then Abram bound the youth with belts and straps,
And builded parapets and trenches there,

And stretched forth the knife to slay his son.
10   When lo! An Angel called him out of heaven,
Saying, Lay not thy hand upon the lad,
Neither do anything to him, thy son.
Behold! Caught in a thicket by its horns,
A Ram. Offer the Ram of Pride instead.

15   But the old man would not so, but slew his son,
And half the seed of Europe, one by one.

Disabled

He sat in a wheeled chair, waiting for dark,
And shivered in his ghastly suit of grey,
Legless, sewn short at elbow. Through the park
Voices of boys rang saddening like a hymn,
5   Voices of play and pleasure after day,
Till gathering sleep had mothered them from him.

* * *

About this time Town used to swing so gay
When glow-lamps budded in the light blue trees,
And girls glanced lovelier as the air grew dim, –
10   In the old times, before he threw away his knees.
Now he will never feel again how slim
Girls' waists are, or how warm their subtle hands.
All of them touch him like some queer disease.

* * *

There was an artist silly for his face,
15   For it was younger than his youth, last year.

Now, he is old; his back will never brace;
He's lost his colour very far from here,
Poured it down shell-holes till the veins ran dry,
And half his lifetime lapsed in the hot race
20   And leap of purple spurted from his thigh.

                        * * *

One time he liked a blood-smear down his leg,
After the matches, carried shoulder-high.
It was after football, when he'd drunk a peg,
He thought he'd better join. – He wonders why.
25   Someone had said he'd look a god in kilts,
That's why; and maybe, too, to please his Meg,
Aye, that was it, to please the giddy jilts
He asked to join. He didn't have to beg;
Smiling they wrote his lie: aged nineteen years.

30   Germans he scarcely thought of; all their guilt,
And Austria's, did not move him. And no fears
Of Fear came yet. He thought of jewelled hilts
For daggers in plaid socks; of smart salutes;
And care of arms; and leave; and pay arrears;
35   *Esprit de corps*; and hints for young recruits.
And soon, he was drafted out with drums and cheers.

                        * * *

Some cheered him home, but not as crowds cheer Goal.
Only a solemn man who brought him fruits
Thanked him; and then enquired about his soul.

                        * * *

40   Now, he will spend a few sick years in institutes,
      And do what things the rules consider wise,
      And take whatever pity they may dole.
      Tonight he noticed how the women's eyes
      Passed from him to the strong men that were whole.
45   How cold and late it is! Why don't they come
      And put him into bed? Why don't they come?

À Terre

(being the philosophy of many soldiers)

      Sit on the bed. I'm blind, and three parts shell.
      Be careful; can't shake hands now; never shall.
      Both arms have mutinied against me, – brutes.
      My fingers fidget like ten idle brats.

5   I tried to peg out soldierly, – no use!
      One dies of war like any old disease.
      This bandage feels like pennies on my eyes.
      I have my medals? – Discs to make eyes close.
      My glorious ribbons? – Ripped from my own back
10   In scarlet shreds. (That's for your poetry book.)

      A short life and a merry one, my buck!
      We used to say we'd hate to live dead-old, –
      Yet now… I'd willingly be puffy, bald,
      And patriotic. Buffers catch from boys
15   At least the jokes hurled at them. I suppose
      Little I'd ever teach a son, but hitting,
      Shooting, war, hunting, all the arts of hurting.
      Well, that's what I learnt, – that, and making money.

Your fifty years ahead seem none too many?
20　Tell me how long I've got? God! For one year
To help myself to nothing more than air!
One Spring! Is one too good to spare, too long?
Spring wind would work its own way to my lung,
And grow me legs as quick as lilac-shoots.

25　My servant's lamed, but listen how he shouts!
When I'm lugged out, he'll still be good for that.
Here in this mummy-case, you know, I've thought
How well I might have swept his floors for ever.
I'd ask no nights off when the bustle's over,
30　Enjoying so the dirt. Who's prejudiced
Against a grimed hand when his own's quite dust,
Less live than specks that in the sun-shafts turn,
Less warm than dust that mixes with arms' tan?
I'd love to be a sweep, now, black as Town,
35　Yes, or a muckman. Must I be his load?

O Life, Life, let me breathe, – a dug-out rat!
Not worse than ours the lives rats lead –
Nosing along at night down some safe rut,
They find a shell-proof home before they rot.
40　Dead men may envy living mites in cheese,
Or good germs even. Microbes have their joys,
And subdivide, and never come to death.
Certainly flowers have the easiest time on earth.
'I shall be one with nature, herb and stone,'
45　Shelley would tell me. Shelley would be stunned:
The dullest Tommy hugs that fancy now.
'Pushing up daisies' is their creed, you know.

To grain, then, go my fat, to buds my sap,
For all the usefulness there is in soap.

50   D'you think the Boche will ever stew man-soup?
Some day, no doubt, if...
                    Friend, be very sure
I shall be better off with plants that share
More peaceably the meadow and the shower.
Soft rains will touch me, – as they could touch once,
55   And nothing but the sun shall make me ware.
Your guns may crash around me. I'll not hear;
Or, if I wince, I shall not know I wince.

Don't take my soul's poor comfort for your jest.
Soldiers may grow a soul when turned to fronds,
60   But here the thing's best left at home with friends.

My soul's a little grief, grappling your chest,
To climb your throat on sobs; easily chased
On other sighs and wiped by fresher winds.

Carry my crying spirit till it's weaned
65   To do without what blood remained these wounds.

Exposure

Our brains ache, in the merciless iced east winds that
    knive us...
Wearied we keep awake because the night is silent...
Low, drooping flares confuse our memory of the salient...
Worried by silence, sentries whisper, curious, nervous,
5   But nothing happens.

Watching, we hear the mad gusts tugging on the wire,
Like twitching agonies of men among its brambles.

Northward, incessantly, the flickering gunnery rumbles,
Far off, like a dull rumour of some other war.
10   What are we doing here?

The poignant misery of dawn begins to grow...
We only know war lasts, rain soaks, and clouds sag
    stormy,
Dawn massing in the east her melancholy army
Attacks once more in ranks on shivering ranks of grey,
15   But nothing happens.

Sudden successive flights of bullets streak the silence.
Less deathly than the air that shudders black with snow,
With sidelong flowing flakes that flock, pause, and renew;
We watch them wandering up and down the wind's
    nonchalance,
20   But nothing happens.

Pale flakes with fingering stealth come feeling for our
    faces –
We cringe in holes, back on forgotten dreams, and
    stare, snow-dazed,
Deep into grassier ditches. So we drowse, sun-dozed,
Littered with blossoms trickling where the blackbird
    fusses.
25   – Is it that we are dying?

Slowly our ghosts drag home: glimpsing the sunk fires,
    glozed
With crusted dark-red jewels; crickets jingle there;
For hours the innocent mice rejoice: the house is theirs;
Shutters and doors, all closed: on us the doors are
    closed, –
30   We turn back to our dying.

Since we believe not otherwise can kind fires burn;
Nor ever suns smile true on child, or field, or fruit.
For God's invincible spring our love is made afraid;
Therefore, not loath, we lie out here; therefore were born,
35   For love of God seems dying.

Tonight, this frost will fasten on this mud and us,
Shrivelling many hands, puckering foreheads crisp.
The burying-party, picks and shovels in shaking grasp,
Pause over half-known faces. All their eyes are ice.
40   But nothing happens.

The Sentry

We'd found an old Boche dug-out, and he knew,
And gave us hell; for shell on frantic shell
Lit full on top, but never quite burst through.
Rain, guttering down in waterfalls of slime,
5   Kept slush waist-high and rising hour by hour,
And choked the steps too thick with clay to climb,
What murk of air remained stank old, and sour
With fumes from whizz-bangs, and the smell of men
Who'd lived there years, and left their curse in the den,
10 If not their corpses...
                         There we herded from the blast
Of whizz-bangs; but one found our door at last, –
Buffeting eyes and breath, snuffing the candles,
And thud! flump! thud! down the steep steps came
      thumping
And sploshing in the flood, deluging muck,
15 The sentry's body; then his rifle, handles
Of old Boche bombs, and mud in ruck on ruck.

We dredged it up, for dead, until he whined,
'O sir – my eyes, – I'm blind, – I'm blind, – I'm blind.'
Coaxing, I held a flame against his lids
20 And said if he could see the least blurred light
He was not blind; in time they'd get all right.
'I can't,' he sobbed. Eyeballs, huge-bulged like squids',
Watch my dreams still, – yet I forgot him there
In posting Next for duty, and sending a scout
25 To beg a stretcher somewhere, and flound'ring about
To other posts under the shrieking air.

Those other wretches, how they bled and spewed,
And one who would have drowned himself for good, –
I try not to remember these things now.
30 Let Dread hark back for one word only: how,
Half-listening to that sentry's moans and jumps,
And the wild chattering of his shivered teeth,
Renewed most horribly whenever crumps
Pummelled the roof and slogged the air beneath, –
35 Through the dense din, I say, we heard him shout
'I see your light!' – But ours had long gone out.

Spring Offensive

Halted against the shade of a last hill
They fed, and eased of pack-loads, were at ease;
And leaning on the nearest chest or knees
Carelessly slept.
                                    But many there stood still
5 To face the stark blank sky beyond the ridge,
Knowing their feet had come to the end of the world.
Marvelling they stood, and watched the long grass
    swirled

By the May breeze, murmurous with wasp and midge;
And though the summer oozed into their veins
10   Like an injected drug for their bodies' pains,
Sharp on their souls hung the imminent ridge of grass,
Fearfully flashed the sky's mysterious glass.

Hour after hour they ponder the warm field
And the far valley behind, where buttercups
15   Had blessed with gold their slow boots coming up;
When even the little brambles would not yield
But clutched and clung to them like sorrowing arms.
They breathe like trees unstirred.

Till like a cold gust thrills the little word
20   At which each body and its soul begird
And tighten them for battle. No alarms
Of bugles, no high flags, no clamorous haste, –
Only a lift and flare of eyes that faced
The sun, like a friend with whom their love is done.
25   O larger shone that smile against the sun, –
Mightier than his whose bounty these have spurned.

So, soon they topped the hill, and raced together
Over an open stretch of herb and heather
Exposed. And instantly the whole sky burned
30   With fury against them; earth set sudden cups
In thousands for their blood; and the green slope
Chasmed and deepened sheer to infinite space.

Of them who running on that last high place
Breasted the surf of bullets, or went up
35   On the hot blast and fury of hell's upsurge,
Or plunged and fell away past this world's verge,
Some say God caught them even before they fell.

But what say such as from existence' brink
Ventured but drave too swift to sink,
40 The few who rushed in the body to enter hell,
And there out-fiending all its fiends and flames
With superhuman inhumanities,
Long-famous glories, immemorial shames –
And crawling slowly back, have by degrees
45 Regained cool peaceful air in wonder –
Why speak not they of comrades that went under?

Selected Letters of Wilfred Owen

Letter 330 To Susan Owen

5 March 1915   *Mérignac*

Dearest of Mothers,

My late letters have been writ for the <u>object</u> thereof; for <u>subjects</u> I lacked. But today I have subject enough [*nine lines missing*]

 Supposing I underwent the rigours, boredom, disgust, danger of Barracks or Camp, or saw Action on the Field,   5
I might have better claim to a Subsidy from my Rich Uncle, which Common Sense, Common Decency, Common Charity are not quite common enough to realize. I say it is a matter of Common Sense. Consider; I ask not for a Defence from Life-Troubles or an Excuse   10
for not labouring, but I ask for a Weapon. I <u>will</u> fight through Life; (have I not fought?) but no headway is to be made without an Arm, whether the Sword that is called Science, or the Munition, Capital. To struggle vulgarly with fist and brick-end, I do refuse. I had rather   15
fall back among the Camp Followers of Life and mend potsherds. My present life, as Father points out, is not leading to anywhere in particular; but situated where I was in 1911, I don't think I could have done wiselier than take the steps I did. True, I have not yet struck out   20
in any direction. Since taking Soundings in Deep Waters, finding them fathomless and terrible, and all but losing my breath there, I have looked out from many observation-towers; and I have lifted the curtains from many a human secrecy.   25

Of the various prospects of the world which I have viewed, I found only one Field in which I could work willingly, and toil without wage. Alas, but we must wait for the waterings of many seasons before hoping to produce therefrom a single acceptable flower! 30

If I study, it will not be, as writes Father, 'to make a comfortable future'. A comfortable future for myself is to be provided for by other means than study. To some, I seem a fellow without a footing in life. But I have my foothold, bold as any, kept for years. A boy, I guessed 35 that the fullest, largest liveable life was that of a Poet. I <u>know</u> it now; but have still to know whether it is the highest and richest: though I begin to think so. Was I born for it? Well, so far, I find myself in possession of a goodly number of birth-certificates to that effect; while 40 I can find only two or three flimsy arguments for the B.A. Craze, and half a dozen sadly unworthy ones for the 'Reverend' pretension. (In measure as I am in darkness, I keep open my ears for the Voice, should it speak. Think not I have stopped my ears to a Call, dear 45 Mother!) But know that my prime object is not to boss a staff of schoolmasters, any more than it is to boom a monster business. There is <u>one</u> title I prize, one clear call audible, one Sphere where I may influence for Truth, one workshop whence I may send forth Beauty, one 50 mode of living entirely congenial to me. In proof, I swear I cannot appreciate any other dignity: Headmaster of Eton; Archbishop of Canterbury; King of the English Race. My ambitions are lesser than Macbeth's and greater, not so happy, but much happier. 55

I said 'in proof'. I should have said 'for evidence'. The real verification is what can I write within say, a year's time? And the Crux is this – that <u>to be able</u> to write as I <u>know how to</u>, study is necessary: a period of study, then

of intercourse with kindred spirits, then of isolation. 60
My heart is ready, but my brain unprepared, and my
hand untrained. And all, – untested. I quite envisage
possibility of non-success.

My hopes rose on a tide of enthusiasm common
enough in youths whose Spring is open to the Sun of 65
Sense and Moon of Melancholy. That tide may now be
about to ebb. Should it be the Tide that leads to Fortune,
miserable me if I take it not at the flood! Shall Poverty
leave me unlaunched? Shall my Timidity bar me? Shall
my Indolence moor me to the mud? 70

Pray, dear Mother, that I may be loosed in time. The
last two shackles are my own task; and now perhaps
I shall forge levers for the First.

One more word: A Captive begs to be set free. Is his
Begging contemptible? Is his supplication comparable to 75
the whine of him who begs to eat? Better to beg boldly
once, than to beg meanly all the rest of one's days.

So saying, I kiss you my own Mother, and confess
I long to see you just as much as I long to see myself as
you would have me. 80

Wilfred

P.S. I like to think you'll keep this letter; as indeed all,
not, of course, megalomaniac's reason; but just because
I keep no Diary; and the landmarks of one's Thoughts
fade away still quicker than Events. You will impart my 85
messages to Father. I never begin 'Dear Mother and
Father' because I have the feeling of addressing an
audience.

P.P.S. I keep unquiet about Harold.

Letter 480 To Susan Owen

Tues 16 January 1917   [*2nd Manchester Regt., B.E.F.*]
My own sweet Mother,
I am sorry you have had about 5 days letterless. I hope
you had my two letters 'posted' since you wrote your
last, which I received tonight. I am bitterly disappointed
that I never got one of yours.

I can see no excuse for deceiving you about these last   5
4 days. I have suffered seventh hell.

I have not been at the front.

I have been in front of it.

I held an advanced post, that is, a 'dug-out' in the
middle of No Man's Land.   10

We had a march of 3 miles over shelled road then
nearly 3 along a flooded trench. After that we came to
where the trenches had been blown flat out and had to
go over the top. It was of course dark, too dark, and the
ground was not mud, not sloppy mud, but an octopus of   15
sucking clay, 3, 4, and 5 feet deep, relieved only by
craters full of water. Men have been known to drown in
them. Many stuck in the mud & only got on by leaving
their waders, equipment, and in some cases their clothes.

High explosives were dropping all around out, and   20
machine guns spluttered every few minutes. But it was
so dark that even the German flares did not reveal us.

Three quarters dead, I mean each of us 3/4 dead, we
reached the dug-out, and relieved the wretches therein. I
then had to go forth and find another dug-out for a still   25
more advanced post where I left 18 bombers. I was
responsible for other posts on the left but there was a
junior officer in charge.

My dug-out held 25 men tight packed. Water filled it
to a depth of 1 or 2 feet, leaving say 4 feet of air.   30

One entrance had been blown in & blocked.

So far, the other remained.

The Germans knew we were staying there and decided we shouldn't.

Those fifty hours were the agony of my happy life.   35

Every ten minutes on Sunday afternoon seemed an hour.

I nearly broke down and let myself drown in the water that was now slowly rising over my knees.

Towards 6 o'clock, when, I suppose, you would be   40
going to church, the shelling grew less intense and less accurate: so that I was mercifully helped to do my duty and crawl, wade, climb and flounder over No Man's Land to visit my other post. It took me half an hour to move about 150 yards.   45

I was chiefly annoyed by our own machine guns from behind. The seeng-seeng-seeng of the bullets reminded me of Mary's canary. On the whole I can support the canary better.

In the Platoon on my left the sentries over the dug-out   50
were blown to nothing. One of these poor fellows was my first servant whom I rejected. If I had kept him he would have lived, for servants don't do Sentry Duty. I kept my own sentries half way down the stairs during the more terrific bombardment. In spite of this one lad   55
was blown down and, I am afraid, blinded.

This was my only casualty.

The officer of the left Platoon has come out completely prostrated and is in hospital.

I am now as well, I suppose, as ever.   60

I allow myself to tell you all these things because <u>I am never going back to this awful post</u>. It is the worst the Manchesters have ever held; and we are going back for a rest.

I hear that the officer who relieved me left his 3 Lewis 65
Guns behind when he came out. (He had only 24 hours
in). He will be court-martialled.

In conclusion, I must say that if there is any power
whom the Soldiery execrate more than another it is that
of our distinguished countryman. You may pass it on 70
via Owen, Owen.

Don't pass round these sheets but have portions
typed for Leslie etc. My previous letter to you has just
been returned. It will be too heavy to include in this.

Your very own Wilfred x 75

Letter 481 To Susan Owen

Friday, 19 January 1917   [*2nd Manchester Regt., B.E.F.*]
We are now a long way back in a ruined village, all
huddled together in a farm. We all sleep in the same
room where we eat and try to live. My bed is a
hammock of rabbit-wire stuck up beside a great shell
hole in the wall. Snow is deep about, and melts through 5
the gaping roof, on to my blanket. We are wretched
beyond my previous imagination – but safe.

Last night indeed I had to 'go up' with a party. We got
lost in the snow. I went on ahead to scout – foolishly
alone – and when half a mile away from the party, got 10
overtaken by
                              GAS
It was only tear-gas from a shell, and I got safely back
(to the party) in my helmet, with nothing worse than a
severe fright! And a few tears, some natural, some
unnatural. 15

Here is an Addition to my List of Wants:

Safety Razor (in my drawer) & Blades
Socks (2 pairs)
6 handkerchiefs
Celluloid Soap Box (Boots)   20
Cigarette Holder (Bone, 3d. or 6d.)
Paraffin for Hair.
(I can't wash hair and have taken to washing my face
with snow.)

Coal, water, candles, accommodation, everything is   25
scarce. We have not always air! When I took my helmet
off last night – O Air it was a heavenly thing!

Please thank Uncle for his letter, and send the Compass.
I scattered abroad some 50 Field Post Cards from the Base,
which should bring forth a good harvest of letters. But   30
nothing but a daily one from you will keep me up.

I think Colin might try a weekly letter. And Father?

We have a Gramophone, and so musical does it seem
now that I shall never more disparage one. Indeed I can
never disparage anything in Blighty again for a long time   35
except certain parvenus living in a street of the same
name as you take to go to the Abbey.

They want to call No Man's Land 'England' because
we keep supremacy there.

It is like the eternal place of gnashing of teeth; the   40
Slough of Despond could be contained in one of its
crater-holes; the fires of Sodom and Gomorrah could
not light a candle to it – to find the way to Babylon the
Fallen.

It is pock-marked like a body of foulest disease and its   45
odour is the breath of cancer.

I have not seen any dead. I have done worse. In the
dank air I have <u>perceived</u> it, and in the darkness, <u>felt</u>.
Those 'Somme Pictures' are the laughing stock of the
army – like the trenches on exhibition in Kensington.   50

No Man's Land under snow is like the face of the moon, chaotic, crater-ridden, uninhabitable, awful, the abode of madness.

To call it 'England'!

I would as soon call my House (!) Krupp Villa, or my   55
child Chlorina Phosgena.

Now I have let myself tell you more facts than I should, in the exuberance of having already done '<u>a Bit</u>.' <u>It is done</u>, and we are all going still farther back for a long time. A long time. The people of England needn't   60
hope. They must agitate. But they are not yet agitated even. Let them imagine 50 strong men trembling as with ague for 50 hours!

Dearer & stronger love than ever. W.E.O.

Letter 482 To Susan Owen

Sunday, 4 February 1917
[*Advanced Horse Transport Depot*]

My own dear Mother,

I am now indeed and in truth very far behind the Line; sent down to this old Town for a Course in Transport Duties. The Battalion did <u>not</u> get out for a rest, and since my last letter I have had another strong dose of the advanced Front Line.   5

To begin with, I have come out quite unhurt, except for a touch of dysentery, which is now passed, and a severe cold and cough which keep me in bed today.

I have no mind to describe all the horrors of this last Tour. But it was almost wusser than the first, because in   10
this place my Platoon had no Dug-Outs, but had to lie in the snow under the deadly wind. By day it was

impossible to stand up or even crawl about because we were behind only a little ridge screening us from the Bosches' periscope. 15

We had 5 Tommy's cookers between the Platoon, but they did not suffice to melt the ice in the water-cans. So we suffered cruelly from thirst.

The marvel is that we did not all die of cold. As a matter of fact, only one of my party actually froze to 20 death before he could be got back, but I am not able to tell how many have ended in hospital. I had no real casualties from shelling, though for 10 minutes every hour whizz-bangs fell a few yards short of us. Showers of soil rained on us, but no fragments of shell could find us. 25

I had lost my gloves in a dug-out, but I found 1 mitten on the Field; I had my Trench Coat (without lining but with a Jerkin underneath.) My feet ached until they could ache no more, and so they temporarily died. I was kept warm by the ardour of Life within me. I forgot 30 hunger in the hunger for Life. The intensity of your Love reached me and kept me living. I thought of you and Mary without a break all the time. I cannot say I felt any fear. We were all half-crazed by the buffeting of the High Explosives. I think the most unpleasant reflection 35 that weighed on me was the impossibility of getting back any wounded, a total impossibility all day, and frightfully difficult by night.

We were marooned on a frozen desert.

There is not a sign of life on the horizon and a 40 thousand signs of death.

Not a blade of grass, not an insect; once or twice a day the shadow of a big hawk, scenting carrion.

By degrees, day by day, we worked back through the reserve, & support lines to the crazy village where the 45 Battalion takes breath. While in Support we inhabited

vast Bosche dug-out (full of all kinds of souvenirs.) They
are so deep that they seem warm like mines! There we
began to thaw. At last I got to the village, & found all
your dear precious letters, and the parcel of good and   50
precious things. The Lamp is perfect your Helmet is
perfect, everything was perfect.

Then I had the heavenly-dictated order to proceed on
a Transport Course. Me in Transports? Aren't <u>you</u>?
When I departed, the gloom among the rest of the Subs.   55
and even among Captains, was a darkness that could be
felt. They can't understand my luck.

It doesn't necessarily mean a job as Transport Officer
straight away, but here I am, in a delightful old town
billeted in a <u>house</u> with a young Scotch Officer.   60

True, we can get no fuel and the very milk freezes in the
jug in a few minutes. True, I am sorely bruised by riding.
True, this kind of Life is expensive. But I have not been so
full of content since the middle of November last.

Tell Colin how we have to ride all manner of   65
horseflesh in the School, cantering round & round for
hours, without stirrups, and folding arms and doing all
kinds of circus tricks.

It is very amusing – to watch.

Tomorrow I shall send a P.C. of this Town which I   70
must not name in a letter.

Address: R.E. Section
  Advanced Horse Transport Depot
   A.P.O. S1.
    BEF France.   75

Hope you had numerous Field P.C.s which I dropped
en route to here.

The Course should last 1 month!!

Alas! I have missed your last letters. It has taken 3 days
to get here.   80

Fondest love to all, & thanks for all their letters,
                              Your own Wilfred x
P.S. I don't at all deserve the spirited approbation which
Father gives me. Though I confess I like to have his kind
letters immensely. I shall read them less shame-facedly in   85
dug-outs and trenches, than I do here in this pleasant
peaceful town.

Quite 10 years ago I made a study of this town
& Cathedral, in the Treasury. It is all familiar now!

Auntie Emma fairly hit it when she 'perceived the   90
awful <u>distaste</u> underlying' my accounts. Dear Aunt was
ever a shrewd Doogie.

I suppose I can endure cold, and fatigue, and the
face-to-face death, as well as another; but extra for me
there is the universal pervasion of <u>Ugliness</u>. Hideous   95
landscapes, vile noises, foul language and nothing but
foul, even from one's own mouth (for all are devil
ridden), everything unnatural, broken, blasted; the
distortion of the dead, whose unburiable bodies sit
outside the dug-outs all day, all night, the most execrable   100
sights on earth. In poetry we call them the most
glorious. But to sit with them all day, all night... and a
week later to come back and find them still sitting there,
in motionless groups, THAT is what saps the 'soldierly
spirit'...   105

Distaste? Distaste, Quotha?

I used to consider Tankerville Street ugly, but now...

Well, I easily forget the unpleasant, and, look you,
I even have to write it down for the sake of future
reminders, reminder of how incomparable is an innocent   110
and quiet life, at home, of work creative or humdrum,
with books or without books, moneyed or moneyless, in
sunshine or fog, but under an inoffensive sky, that does
not shriek all night with flights of shells.

Again I have said too much. But let me repeat that I   115
am mighty snug here, and have a goodly prospect before
me now.

I am not sorry you keep in bed from time to time, but I do
hope you'll soon get some sunny walks. Are you painting?

The Letter from Lancs. was from Bobby. All the   120
brothers are in college there. Miss de la Touche is as
Bobby says 'supposed to be boss' of a Belgian Hospital
in London.

Again, dearest love to all. W.E.O.

Letter 664 To Siegfried Sassoon

10 October 1918   [*2nd Manchester Regt.*]
Very dear Siegfried,
Your letter reached me at the exact moment it was most
needed – when we had come far enough out of the line
to feel the misery of billets; and I had been seized with
writer's cramp after making out my casualty reports.
(I'm O.C. D Coy).   5

The Batt. had a sheer time last week. I can find no
better epithet: because I cannot say I suffered anything;
having let my brain grow dull: That is to say my nerves
are in perfect order.

It is a strange truth: that your *Counter-Attack*   10
frightened me much more than the real one: though the
boy by my side, shot through the head, lay on top of me,
soaking my shoulder, for half an hour.

Catalogue? Photograph? Can you photograph the
crimson-hot iron as it cools from the smelting? That is   15
what Jones's blood looked like, and felt like. My senses
are charred.

I shall feel again as soon as I dare, but now I must not. I don't take the cigarette out of my mouth when I write Deceased over their letters.

But one day I will write Deceased over many books.

I'm glad I've been recommended for M.C., & hope I get it, for the confidence it may give me at home. Full of confidence after having taken a few machine guns (with the help of one seraphic lance corporal,) I held a most glorious brief peace talk in a pill box. You would have been '*en pamoisons*'.

I found one of your poems in another L. Cpl's possession! The Theosophist one it was: containing, let me tell you, the one line I resent.

> In bitter safety I awake unfriended.
> Please apologise – now.

. . .

I have nothing to tell you except that I'm rather glad my servant was happily wounded: & so away from me. He had lived in London, a Londoner.

While you are apparently given over to wrens, I have found brave companionship in a poppy, behind whose stalk I took cover from five machine-guns and several howitzers.

I desire no more <u>exposed flanks</u> of any sort for a long time.

Of many who promised to send me literary magazines no one has succeeded, except the Ed. of *Today* who sent me (by whose request?) Mais's article & the picture, which I have at last managed to stick to the corrugated iron wall of my Tamboo. For mercy's sake send me something to read which may help to neutralize my present stock of literature. I send you the choicest of specimens.

Ever your W.E.O.

Letter 673 To Susan Owen

Thurs. 31 October [*1918*] *6.15 p.m.*

[*2nd Manchester Regt.*]

Dearest Mother,

I will call the place from which I'm now writing 'The Smoky Cellar of the Forester's House'. I write on the first sheet of the writing pad which came in the parcel yesterday. Luckily the parcel was small, as it reached me just before we moved off to the line. Thus only the paraffin was unwelcome in my pack. My servant & I ate the chocolate in the cold middle of last night, crouched under a draughty Tamboo, roofed with planks. I husband the Malted Milk for tonight, & tomorrow night. The handkerchief & socks are most opportune, as the ground is marshy, & I have a slight cold!

So thick is the smoke in this cellar that I can hardly see by a candle 12 ins. away, and so thick are the inmates that I can hardly write for pokes, nudges & jolts. On my left the Coy. Commander snores on a bench: other officers repose on wire beds behind me. At my right hand, Kellett, a delightful servant of A Coy. in <u>The Old Days</u> radiates joy & contentment from pink cheeks and baby eyes. He laughs with a signaller, to whose left ear is glued the Receiver; but whose eyes rolling with gaiety show that he is listening with his right ear to a merry corporal, who appears at this distance away (some three feet nothing [but] a gleam of white teeth & a wheeze of jokes.

Splashing my hand, an old soldier with a walrus moustache peels & drops potatoes into the pot. By him, Keyes, my cook, chops wood; another feeds the smoke with the damp wood.

It is a great life. I am more oblivious than alas!

yourself, dear Mother, of the ghastly glimmering of the 30
guns outside, & the hollow crashing of the shells.

There is no danger down here, or if any, it will be well
over before you read these lines.

I hope you are as warm as I am; as serene in your room
as I am here; and that you think of me never in bed as 35
resignedly as I think of you always in bed. Of this I am
certain you could not be visited by a band of friends half
so fine as surround me here.

Ever Wilfred x

Notes on the Poems

Sonnet

Written at Teignmouth, on a Pilgrimage to Keats's House

In April 1911, Owen began to be passionately excited by the work of John Keats, a major influence in his early poems. On a visit to Torquay in Devon, Owen bought a biography of the poet and

> ... began this morning 'with fear and trembling' to learn the details of his life. I sometimes feel in reading such books that I would give ten years of life to have been born a hundred years earlier.
>
> **(Letter 79 to Susan Owen, *SL*, page 15)**

Learning that Keats had lived at nearby Teignmouth for several months in 1818, Owen went on a 'pilgrimage' to see the house where he had lived. He 'gaped at it (regardless of people in the window who finally became quite alarmed, I fancy)' (Letter 80 to Susan Owen, *SL*, page 16).

2 Keats's own letters had been full of complaints about the Devonshire weather. In this sonnet, Owen describes a suitably sombre day for mourning the young poet. Keats died at the age of 25, as Owen would himself.

8 Keats's tomb is in Rome. He asked that it should be inscribed: 'Here lies one whose name was writ in water.'

Nocturne

Written in the summer of 1915, when Owen was staying at Mérignac, France, *Nocturne* reflects Owen's interest in the style and ideas of the younger poets of the Romantic era. The mood and diction reflect the influence of Keats. For example, compare the opening of Keats's famous *Ode to a Nightingale*: 'My heart aches and a drowsy numbness pains/My sense...'

However, rather than a romantic picture of night, *Nocturne* offers instead a social protest against harsh, industrial work conditions. The poet prays that all those who are *a-weary seeking bread* will find rest. His fears that there are *too many* workers who *cannot dream* prevent him from sleeping peacefully himself.

A nocturne can be either a piece of music written to evoke the beauty of night, or a set of prayers to be said at night. To what extent is Owen's poem like either of these?

Happiness

Begun at Abbeville, France, in February 1917, soon after Owen's first experience of the battlefront, this sonnet is, in a way, an 'exercise'. He had an arrangement with his cousin, Leslie Gunston, and a friend, Olwen Joergens, that they would set each other titles for sonnets and send each other their work for criticism. Joergens chose the title *Happiness*.

The poem explores feelings of sadness at the loss of the kind of innocent 'pure' happiness that belongs with childhood and home. It also suggests the loss of simple religious faith.

5–6 These lines are rather mysterious, but Owen sent the poem to his mother with a letter:

My 'Happiness' is dedicated to you. It contains perhaps two good <u>lines</u>. Between you an' me the sentiment is all bilge. Or nearly all. But I think it makes a creditable Sonnet. You must not conclude I

have misbehaved in any way from the tone of the poem... On
the contrary I have been a very good boy.

(Letter 487, 25 February 1917, *SL*, page 223)

12–14   Six months later, Owen was to describe the first draft of these
lines as 'his first mature work', saying that the maturity had
come from his experience of the Front at Beaumont Hamel
(Hibberd, *Wilfred Owen*, page 280).

Inspection

The speaker in this poem is an officer, carrying out an inspection
of his platoon, something which Owen would have had to do
regularly. In June 1916 he writes of his first experience of this:

... Had to assist inspection of kit, this morning.
... I see a toothbrush and a box of polish missing. I demand in a
terrible voice 'Where's your TOOTH-BRUSH?' and learn that the
fellow has just returned from 'overseas'!

(Letter 439, 19 June 1916, *SL*, page 188)

The poem was written at Craiglockhart, in August and September
1917. The influence of Siegfried Sassoon can be seen in the use of
realistic, colloquial slang in the soldiers' dialogue and the bitterly
ironic tone.

   7   **damnèd spot**   In Shakespeare's *Macbeth* (V.i), Lady Macbeth
says 'Out, damnèd spot' as she sleepwalks, repeatedly trying in
her nightmare to wash her hands of the blood of King
Duncan, whom she has murdered. What she is trying to get
rid of is the guilt that haunts her.
  15   **white-washed**   has three layers of meaning. First, it describes
the pale, washed-out faces of dead men; white-washing was
also carried out on army buildings to make them look better
for inspections; it also refers ironically to the idea that the
truth about the war was being covered up or 'whitewashed' by
senior officials.

Anthem for Doomed Youth

This sonnet was written in September–October 1917, at Craiglockhart War Hospital. Siegfried Sassoon, who helped Owen with the revision of the poem, was impressed by its 'classic and imaginative serenity'. On 25 September, Owen wrote to his mother: 'I send you my two best war Poems. Sassoon supplied the title "Anthem": just what I meant it to be.'

The poem bitterly contrasts the traditional rituals that were used to mark a death in civilian life with the inevitable lack of ceremony for the victims of mass slaughter in war. Bells, prayers, choirs singing the requiem, candles, the pall (the cloth spread over a coffin), flowers and the old tradition of closing the blinds or curtains in a house where there has been a death are all given their ironic equivalents in the sights and sounds of the battlefield. Aural imagery, such as alliteration, vividly evokes the horrific noises that surround the dead and dying men; for example, in *the stuttering rifles' rapid rattle*.

The mood alters in the sestet, becoming poignant and subdued. Owen asks what sort of ceremony is even possible in these circumstances. The answer seems to be that it is the responses of the families mourning their dead that are important, rather than rituals that seem mere *mockeries*. Owen may have been thinking of his own family when he imagined boys with *glimmers* of tears in their eyes, the pale faces of the girls and the tender thoughts of the bereaved.

The last glimmers of light in the eyes of the dying take the place of candles.

1 **passing-bells** funeral bells.
  cattle suggests slaughter in the abattoir, emphasizing the dehumanizing, undignified nature of death in battle and the 'herds' of victims.
4 **orisons** prayers.
5 **mockeries** Some soldiers were given hasty burial

ceremonies, which may have seemed like mockeries, but Owen is probably suggesting that any religious ritual becomes a mockery in the face of such indiscriminate slaughter.

6–7 Echoes Keats's *To Autumn*: 'Then in a wailful choir the small gnats mourn.'

9 **to speed them**   to help them on their way to death, or perhaps to help their souls on their way to heaven.

14 The dusk falls each evening, shutting out the light, like a metaphorical closing of the blinds in mourning for the deaths that have occurred that day. Compare this with lines from Laurence Binyon's *For the Fallen*, a poem that romanticizes death in battle far more than Owen does here: 'At the going down of the sun and in the morning/We will remember them'.

Maundy Thursday

Originally drafted in France in 1915, this poem was revised late in 1917. While he was working in France, Owen was invited to spend holidays with friends or with the families of students. With them he sometimes attended 'High mass: real genuine Mass, with candle, with book, and with bell, and all like abominations of desolation', though he was careful to tell his mother that, 'always I come out from these performances an hour and a half older: <u>otherwise unchanged</u>' (Letter 336 to Susan Owen, *SL*, page 147). In this poem, Owen describes the Easter ritual of 'The Veneration of the Cross' – which takes place on Good Friday rather than on Maundy Thursday – where each member of the congregation comes forward to kiss an effigy of Christ on the cross. When the speaker comes to take his turn, he chooses to kiss the *warm live hand* holding the cross, rather than the cold, dead image of Christ. It seems that Owen was rejecting old rituals that seemed dead and meaningless to him, and embracing instead life and humanity.

The poem shows the influence of the 'aesthetic' or 'decadent' poets, popular in France and England in the late nineteenth century. It is typical of their approach to challenge orthodox views, or even to shock, by taking religious subject matter, such as this, and presenting it purely for aesthetic effect, as a beautiful or sensual experience rather than a spiritual one.

On My Songs

Although the final version of this sonnet dates from 1917, it was initially drafted in January 1913, at what was a troubled time for Owen. He had been living at Dunsden vicarage and working as a Parish Assistant, but found the evangelical, Revivalist approach to religion stifling and oppressive and began to doubt whether it was a true expression of Christianity. The vicar may even have forbidden him to write poetry. He sent the first draft of the poem in a letter to his mother, telling her that he wanted desperately to 'escape from this hotbed of religion' (Letter 172, 4 January 1913, *SL*, page 68). He felt this connected him with 'the immortals of earthly Fame', the Romantic poets such as Shelley and Coleridge, who had run 'away from College' to escape 'overbearing elders'.

> Only where in me is the mighty Power of Verse that covered the multitude of their sins. It is true I still find great comfort in scribbling; but lately I am deadening to all poetic impulses, save those due to the pressure of Problems pushing me to seek relief in unstopping my mouth.
>
> (Letter 172, 4 January 1913)

He doubts his own abilities, but still finds it therapeutic to write.

The poem tells of how he has found it comforting to read the work of other poets, who seem to understand and find words to express his sorrows. Sometimes, though, they offer nothing that fits or helps. Then he has to soothe himself, by putting his *weird reveries* into words and writing his own poems, like a *motherless child* who has to sing himself to sleep. He concludes with the hope that his poems might bring comfort to others in the future, in the same way that earlier poets had helped him.

A few months earlier he had been inspired by a sonnet *To the Spirit of Keats* by the American poet James Russell Lowell, telling his mother, 'Except for its merits of expression, I might have done it myself'.

'Great soul, thou sittest with me in my room,
Uplifting me with thy vast quiet eyes,
On whose full orbs with kindly lustre, lies
The twilight warmth of ruddy ember-gloom.
Thy clear strong tones will oft bring sudden bloom
Of hope secure to him who lonely cries,
Wrestling with the young poet's agonies,
Neglect and scorn, which seem a certain doom.'
    (quoted in Letter 157, 17 September 1912, *SL*, page 65)

12 **in this Sick Room**   in a similar state of unhappiness.
14 **haply**   perhaps.

1914

This was perhaps Owen's first poem about the war. It was drafted in autumn 1914, when he was working as an English tutor in Bordeaux, France. He revised the poem late in 1917, when his view of the war was very different, but he chose to leave it much as it was.

Though the war 'sometimes nagged at his conscience' (Hibberd, *Wilfred Owen*, page 188) and he responded with sadness and anger to news of casualties, as yet the war had had little direct impact on him. His language here is conventionally poetic and abstract and the poem presents a view of the war that was quite commonly expressed in the early stages: that it was part of an inevitable natural cycle of death and renewal. As with the seasons, human civilization has passed through its spring and summer, with the flowering of the classical civilizations of ancient Greece and Rome. Now autumn is giving way to winter, with destruction and devastation clearing the way for something new to arise in another *Spring*. This view of civilization is typical of the 'Decadent' movement.

> 1 In *The Revolt of Islam*, ix, line 25, Shelley had written: 'This is the Winter of the World; – and here/We die'.
> 3–6 In this metaphor of the ship of 'Progress' in a great storm, Germany is seen as the evil, aggressive power at the centre of the destruction of European civilization and Art.

It is interesting to compare this sonnet with Rupert Brooke's famous cycle of patriotic sonnets *1914*, which was published in December 1914 and became hugely popular. However, Owen's poem was written earlier and any apparent slight similarities are probably coincidental.

I Saw His Round Mouth's Crimson

In this short and strangely beautiful poem, a man's death is compared to a sunset and the onset of night. The imagery is very sensual, echoing traditional love poetry in its description of the dying man's face and features, yet it also has a solemn, impersonal and almost mystical quality. The *cold stars* reflected in his eyes make him seem remote, looking into the *different skies* of death.

Some critics consider this may be only a fragment intended to be part of a longer poem, but others find it complete and effective in itself. It was probably written at Scarborough in November–December 1917.

> 7 **cold star** Compare *Futility*, line 9 (page 36).

Apologia pro Poemate Meo

The title means 'In Defence of my Poetry'. The poem, written late in 1917, is thought to have been a response to a comment in a letter from Robert Graves: 'For God's sake cheer up and write more optimistically... a poet should have a spirit above wars' (quoted in Hibberd, *Wilfred Owen*, page 369). There are also echoes of Graves's poem *Two Fusiliers*. Owen is justifying his often grim, pessimistic portrayals of war.

On one draft of the poem he quoted, not quite correctly, from the French pacifist writer Henri Barbusse: 'If there be a bright side to war, it is a crime to exhibit it' (Hibberd, *Wilfred Owen*, page 369). What is your response to this idea?

The poem makes the point that writing optimistically about war could be misleading to civilians, giving those who had not experienced the trenches the impression that soldiers were happy with their lot. Yes, soldiers may find laughter and feel excitement or even exultation in the heat of battle; they may experience love and fellowship or comradeship; but, Owen says, *he* is not going to express any of this to outsiders. *He* is not going to write anything in his poems that might suggest to civilians that soldiers are *well content*. The only people who should be allowed to *hear their mirth* are those who will truly understand because they have been at the Front themselves and shared *With them in hell the sorrowful dark of hell*. Others are not worthy. Although the wording of the title might suggest it, the tone of the poem is far from apologetic. The reader (or the 'you' to whom the poem is addressed) is put firmly in his or her place: 'You are not worth their merriment.'

10 **barrage**   a continuous shower of heavy firing that formed a barrier behind which soldiers could move or advance.

12 **entanglement**   the barbed wire used to deter enemy advances.

15 **oblation** a sacrifice or religious offering.

16 **Seraphic** angelic; a six-winged celestial being, the seraph was an angel of the highest status.

17–20 The love of soldiers is not romantic like the love in the *old song* of traditional poetry; Owen's cousin Leslie Gunston had written of *the binding of fair lips* in a sentimental love poem.

26 **hoarse oaths** the swearing of men trying to encourage each other and keep their spirits up.

At a Calvary near the Ancre

War poets quite frequently related the suffering of soldiers to Christ's sacrifice on the cross. Here the story of the crucifixion is used to attack the hypocrisy of priests who were sent to the battlefront by the Church. They are accused of taking *pride* in their own slight wounds – in being *flesh-marked* – while the soldiers are being 'crucified' around them. To the priests, *The Beast* is Germany; but Owen is also suggesting that they carry the marks of the Devil, who was said to leave his fingermarks on the flesh of his followers. This Devil is War. In supporting the war, the priests are completely denying *gentle Christ's* teachings that we should 'Love one another' and 'Love your enemies'. Owen had realized that 'pure Christianity will not fit in with pure patriotism' (see Interpretations, pages 120–121). The poem was probably written at Craiglockhart, in October 1917.

Title **Calvary** is the name of the place where Jesus was crucified; it means 'The place of the skull'. A calvary is also a model or statue of Christ on the cross, found at many wayside shrines or crossroads in France.

Ancre Owen had arrived at the Front near the river Ancre, a tributary of the Somme, in January 1917. The horrific conditions and the beginning of his disillusionment are described in his letters. (See Letter 480, 16 January 1917, on page 54.)

3 When Jesus was crucified, his *disciples* hid, in fear for their own lives.

4 **Soldiers** kept watch at the cross as Jesus was dying.

5 **Golgotha** another name for Calvary. *Priests* and *scribes* scorned Jesus as he passed.

10 Some priests sent out to the Front expressed support for the government and used religion to justify the war. Compare the way they *shove* and *bawl* with the gentleness of the last two lines.

12 'Greater love hath no man than this, that a man lay down his life for his friends' (John 15:13). See also *Greater Love*, page 36.

Miners

On 12 January 1918, an explosion at the Podmore Hall Colliery, Halmerend, Staffordshire, killed 155 miners, many of them teenage boys who had only recently started work. This was headline news and obviously made an impression on Owen, who quickly responded with this poem, written at Scarborough on 14 January. He sent it to the editor of *The Nation*, a weekly paper open to publishing work critical of the war, and it appeared in print on 26 January. Owen was paid two guineas – 'my first proud earnings'.

Although 'Miners' is not primarily a war poem, Owen told Sassoon that he got 'mixed up with the war at the end'. Sitting by the fire, he imagines the coal whispering to him of its natural origins, in *Frond-forests* deep in the prehistoric past. Instead, the coals tell of the mine and of the men and boys who have suffered and died there. In the ashes he sees the *white bones* of countless men, whose sacrifice is usually forgotten. Not surprisingly, this leads him, in stanza 6, to thoughts of *all that worked dark pits/Of war*. He may be referring particularly to those who worked as 'sappers', tunnelling under No Man's Land or enemy lines to set mines (as imagined by Sebastian Faulks in *Birdsong*) but the words could apply equally well to soldiers in the trenches or all men involved in the war.

In the final two stanzas, he includes himself among them. He imagines people far in the future, warm and comfortable, oblivious of the fate of either miners or soldiers, who... *will not dream of us poor lads,/Left in the ground* (33–4).

Notice the consistent use of pararhyme here. When the poem was published, this technique was still considered quite unconventional and original in English poetry. Owen's cousin Leslie Gunston complained that it offended his 'musical ear'. (See also Interpretations, 'Pararhyme', page 136).

8 **fauns**   In ancient Roman mythology, a faun was a minor god of the forest, with the body of a man and the horns, ears, tail and hind legs of a goat.

17 **cinder-shard**   broken pieces of the burnt-out remains of coal.

26 **amber**   Its golden yellow colour suggests warmth and richness, but it also has a link with coal as both are fossilized substances.

29–34 The six-line stanza adds extra emphasis to the idea that the 'lads' are forgotten – they are outside the pattern, tacked on like an afterthought.

34 **Left**   In *The Nation* this was replaced with 'Lost' and other minor changes were made, at the suggestion of Siegfried Sassoon. Which option do you find more effective?

Dulce et Decorum Est

This famous and often-quoted poem is a powerful protest addressed to those who wrote recruiting literature that represented war as honourable or sporting. Initially it carried an ironic dedication to Jessie Pope, or 'A Certain Poetess', who was responsible for many enthusiastic, patriotic verses. The title of one of her books, *Simple Rhymes for Stirring Times*, gives an idea of the tone of her work. In *The Call*, for example, she contrasts the 'laddie' who is 'going out to win' with a coward who would rather 'save his skin' (see Reilly, *Scars Upon My Heart*, page 88).

The title and final lines of the poem quote sarcastically from the Roman poet Horace. Owen wrote to his mother in October 1917:

> Here is a gas poem, done yesterday, (which is not private, but not final).
> The famous Latin tag means of course <u>It is sweet and meet to die for one's country</u>. <u>Sweet</u>! And <u>decorous</u>!
>
> (Letter 552, ?16 October 1917, *SL*, page 283)

Owen goes to great lengths to show war at its least 'decorous', describing decrepit men staggering through the mud and the gruesome death of a victim of gas poisoning, which he can't erase from his memory. If Jessie Pope, or others like her, could see what he has seen, they would not be so ready to promote *The old Lie*.

   1–8 The description of the exhausted soldiers makes a striking contrast with images of men marching to battle in poems written early in the war, such as Laurence Binyon's *For the Fallen* (September 1914):

> They went with songs to the battle, they were young,
> Straight of limb, true of eye, steady and aglow.
> They were staunch to the end against odds uncounted,
> They fell with their faces to the foe.
>
> (*Oxford Book of War Poetry*, ed. Jon Stallworthy, page 209)

     See Owen's letters of January and February 1917 (pages 54–62) for an account of the conditions endured by men at the Front.

   8 **Five-Nines** 5.9 calibre explosive shells.

   9 **Gas** mustard gas, one of the first forms of chemical warfare, was introduced at the Battle of Ypres in 1915. It burns the membranes of the throat and lungs. Many soldiers were

Notes

poisoned and died an agonizing death, much as Owen describes in the remainder of the poem.

10–11 Gas masks were supplied, but they were heavy and cumbersome and one man has failed to fit his quickly enough.

12 **lime**   white, caustic earth used as fertilizer; bird-lime was a sticky substance used for catching birds; both have connotations here.

13–14 The gas masks had celluloid windows, giving the effect of being underwater, like a deep-sea diver.

15 The poem was written at Craiglockhart, where Owen, like other shell-shocked soldiers, probably suffered from flashbacks or recurring nightmares.

17–25 **you... My friend**   Jessie Pope – or anyone who presents war as glorious and honourable.

21–4 The description of the symptoms of mustard gas poisoning is as repulsive as Owen could make it. Do you think he goes too far?

The Dead-Beat

Soon after Owen first met Siegfried Sassoon at Craiglockhart, he wrote this poem in Sassoon's satirical style. He describes an exhausted, or perhaps shell-shocked, soldier in a state of collapse, and the unsympathetic responses of his fellow soldiers, an officer and a doctor, who all think he is *malingering*. The officer relates the incident in the everyday colloquial language of soldiers. The traumatized man, *stupid like a cod*, seems deliberately unappealing. What is your response to him?

In stanza 2, another voice, *low* and more compassionate, intervenes, suggesting the man is not scared of the fighting, but demoralized by the thought of people back home going on with their lives while he is forgotten. He seems to have lost the will to live. Later, the man dies, despite being *Unwounded*. As a victim of shell-shock himself Owen had some empathy for those who broke down and could no longer fight, despite no outer signs of injury, though here he speaks in the persona of the unsympathetic officer. The dismissive words of the doctor are based on a real incident. Owen wrote 'These are the very words!' on a draft he sent to his cousin.

    6 **blasted** literally destroyed, and also slang, as the soldier curses the trench.

    9 **Blighty** Soldiers' slang for Britain, and also for a wound that was not life-threatening, but severe enough to warrant being sent home.

    pluck courage.

10–11 **valiant** A sarcastic reference to older men or relatives who have encouraged him to fight, safe in the knowledge that they are too old to be called up themselves.

12–13 **brave** Similarly, this sarcastically imagines his wife, newly widowed, quickly re-marrying someone with more money.

    14 **stiffs** corpses.

    Hun Soldiers' slang for the Germans.

    16 **strafe** bombardment.

Insensibility

This poem explores various ways in which men become 'insensible', or lose their power to feel, when exposed to the horrors of war. It is a useful defence, Owen suggests, enabling men to survive the unbearable. In stanzas 4 and 5, however, he places himself apart from the ordinary soldier or *the lad whose mind was never trained*. As a poet, he sees himself among the *wise*, who retain their sensitivity and can be overwhelmed by *a thought*. He seems to assume that those less well educated than he is do not have the same powers of imagination or ability to feel pain. Finally, he angrily curses those who have not been to war, but have made themselves insensible *By choice* and who feel no pity for the suffering of the soldiers.

Written in the form of a Pindaric Ode, *Insensibility* may be a response to poems by Wordsworth, either *Character of the Happy Warrior* or the *Immortality Ode*, which explore the theme of loss of imagination. Notice the contrast of the repeated *Happy...* with the way the poem turns – *But* – in stanza 6. Look carefully also at the effect of the way pararhyme is used in combination with uneven line lengths. (For 'pararhyme' see Interpretations, page 136.)

The poem was probably drafted at Craiglockhart late in 1917 and revised in April 1918.

3 **fleers**   mocks.

5 **alleys cobbled with their brothers**   In March 1918, Owen mentioned in a letter that the second battle of the Somme was raging over the same ground 'which already in 1916 was cobbled with skulls' (Letter 605 to Mary Owen, *SL*, page 319).

7–11 **flowers... but no one bothers**   A bitter contrast between poets' romantic concern with death and the impersonal attitude to lost troops who are no longer individuals, but mere *gaps for filling*.

15–16 **tease and doubt... Chance**   The only way to cope with the constant uncertainty about whether they would live or die was to shut off their feelings.

17 **shilling**   Soldiers' pay; it was traditional for recruiting officers to give newly enlisted soldiers what was known as 'The King's Shilling'.

23 **all things red**   every gruesome death or wound possible.

28–9 **cautery... ironed**   In the treatment of wounds, a hot iron implement can be used to burn out, or cauterize, infected tissue or to destroy nerve-endings so that pain is no longer felt.

37 **taciturn**   reluctant to speak; silent.

40 **besmirch**   smear, soil.

43 **blunt and lashless**   The ordinary soldier's vision is straightforward, not like that of the sensitive poet, who might, stereotypically, have long eyelashes. Owen once described the look on soldiers' faces as 'more terrible than terror... like a dead rabbit's.'

44 **vital** living.

49 **old men's placidity** the young soldier who is desensitized has an apparent sense of calm acceptance you would only expect to find in an old man.

50 **dullards** dull-witted, stupid people.

53 **paucity** small-mindedness; lack of imagination – very different from simplicity.

59 **reciprocity** Merryn Williams suggests that Owen's 'passionate belief is that "reciprocity" – instinctive sympathy, often expressed through tears – is an essential human duty' (Williams, *Wilfred Owen*, page 86). (See Interpretations, page 114.)

Strange Meeting

This famous poem was described by Siegfried Sassoon as Owen's 'passport to immortality'. It is a moving exploration of the dreamlike fantasy that, after death and in Hell, the poet encounters an enemy soldier he has killed. The man speaks to him of *The pity of war*, the loss of their potential as poets, of what they might have achieved in life, against the backdrop of the wider trends they are powerless to prevent. Because of their deaths, the truth about war will remain *untold* and nations will not learn the lessons of war. The young soldiers may have been 'enemies', but what they have in common goes beyond nationality, to the heart of what it means to be human. *I am the enemy you killed, my friend*: this poignant line sums up the waste and pointlessness of war. Owen drafted the poem early in 1918.

The ideas and images here show that Owen was still very much under the influence of the Romantic poets. Passages from Shelley's long poem, *The Revolt of Islam*, written 1828–32, show clear similarities. Compare this account of two enemy soldiers meeting after a battle:

> And one whose spear had pierced me, leaned beside,
> With quivering lips and humid eyes; – and all
> Seemed like some brothers on a journey wide
> Gone forth, whom now strange meeting did befall.
>
> (Shelley, *The Revolt of Islam*)

Read the poem aloud to hear the effect of the consistent and rhythmic use of pararhyme.

2–3 The strange, underground landscape of Hell has parallels in the work of Shelley and Keats as well as recalling the literal use of mines and tunnels in the First World War. It can also be interpreted as the narrator's unconscious mind.

   3 **titanic** gigantic; the Titans were the oldest of the Ancient Greek gods.

   4 **encumbered** burdened, weighed down; describing those who suffer in Hell.

  13 **flues** air ducts, which functioned like chimneys, to take smoke out from tunnels or dugouts.

17–19 The enemy soldier seems to have shared the same dreams of seeking beauty, which lies in poetry rather than in girls with *braided hair*.

  25 See Owen's Preface, on page 19.

  29 After the war, nations will continue to *trek* in the opposite direction from progress and no one will challenge this.

  33 **vain citadels** fortresses that offer no real safety or protection; the world will 'retreat' behind concepts such as glory and honour that disguise the real nature of war.

  36 He believes there are still some truths and ideals that cannot be corrupted.

  38 **cess** sewage; filth.

  39 Suggests that mental and spiritual suffering can be as real as physical wounds.

Arms and the Boy

Owen placed this poem under the heading 'Protest – the unnaturalness of weapons' in the draft contents list for the book he hoped to publish. The emphasis here is on the contrast between the vicious killing properties of the weapons and the innocence of the boy who is being trained to use them. The poem was written at Ripon in May 1918.

The bayonet-blades in stanza 1 and the bullets in stanza 2 are personified as full of desire to *nuzzle* and penetrate the bodies of their victims. What does alliteration contribute to the effect of the descriptions of the weapons?

The third stanza suggests that there are no signs that this young man is going to become like a devil – with claws or horns – yet he will soon be using hellish weapons.

The title of the poem may refer to *Arms and the Man* (1894), a play by George Bernard Shaw which is critical of militarism. Originally the phrase comes from the opening sentence of *The Aeneid*, by the Latin poet Virgil: 'Arma virumque cano' (I sing of arms and a man).

4 **famishing**   starving.
11 **talons**   hooked claws, as of a bird of prey.
12 His thick curls make him sound little more than a child.

The Show

Relentlessly bleak, this poem presents a grim, aerial view of a battle on the Western Front. Accompanied by the personification of Death, the narrator's soul surveys the scene from a height. He describes a grotesque, diseased landscape in which lines of advancing troops, which look from above like long caterpillars writhing in agony, destroy and 'eat' each other. Finally, he falls to earth, where Death shows him one of the 'worms' with its head severed. This proves to be his own head. Commanding his platoon, Owen would have been literally at its head during single-file advances. Possibly the image relates to his experience in April 1917, when a shell exploded close to him. Although he was not wounded, he was knocked out and separated from the men he was leading. This incident caused the shell shock which led to his repatriation to Craiglockhart. The poem has the dreamlike quality of shock, as if the narrator is dissociated, or distanced from his bodily experience.

Initially entitled 'Vision', the poem was drafted in November 1917, when Owen had recently been 'set alight' by the prize-winning war novel *Le Feu*, by the French writer Henri Barbusse. Its first chapter is entitled 'The Vision' and includes similar birds'-eye images of the trenches: 'Dwarfed to the size of insects and worms, they make a queer dark stirring among these shadow-hidden and Death-pacified lands' (quoted by Stallworthy in *The Poems of Wilfred Owen*, 1985, page 133).

This was one of Owen's first war poems to make consistent and effective use of pararhyme. In a letter to Siegfried Sassoon, he asks, 'What do you think of my Vowel-rime stunt, in this [À Terre] and "Vision"?'

Title   During the First World War, 'Show' was soldiers' slang for battle. Here, the narrator sees the battle from a distance, as if watching a performance. The quotation from Yeats's poetic drama *The Shadowy Waters* (1906) is used ironically, with the word 'tarnished' in place of the original 'burnished'. It refers to 'ever-living' Gods who create humans and then indifferently watch their suffering.

3–5   Compare Owen's use of language in his letter of 19 January 1917 (on page 57), where he describes the appearance of No Man's Land. The desolation is so great that he struggles to find images strong enough to convey the horror of it.

3   **dearth**   famine; the barren landscape is sick and feverish as if from starvation.

6 **beard... wire**   the coils of barbed wire used as barricades at
the Front.

17 **Brown... grey**   The British troops wear khaki, the Germans
grey. The *bristling spines* are the spiked helmets of the Germans.

18 The 'caterpillars' – or troops – have come from green
countryside; it seems unnatural that they should be so *intent* on
coming into this sick landscape of mud.

19 **spawn**   The German troops appear to multiply more quickly –
like fish or frogs producing masses of eggs.

20 **Ramped**   as in 'rampaged'; attacked with violent aggression.

Futility

In his letter of 4 February 1917 (on page 58) describing the
freezing conditions that probably inspired *Exposure* (page 45),
Owen relates that 'only one of my party actually froze to death
before he could be got back'. In this despairing poem, as the sun
rises on a snowy morning soldiers try to rouse a dead comrade.
If the sun has the power to create life on earth, surely its warmth
can wake this one man. The dead youth becomes a symbol of all
the war's waste of young lives. Bitterly, the poem asks whether
there is any point to life on earth, if this is to be the outcome.

3 **half-sown**   Earlier editions read 'unsown'. The young man
may be a farmer who used to rise with the sun to sow his seed,
but whose land now remains uncultivated; the *half-sown* fields
may represent his unlived life in a more general sense.

9 **cold star**   the Earth; the warmth of the sun brought life to the
planet.

10 **dear achieved**   So much effort goes into the creation and
nurturing of life, how can it be thrown away so lightly? Women,
who gave birth to and reared sons only to lose them in the war,
were particularly aware of the tragedy of this.

12 It is bitterly ironic that human life, which has evolved so far
from the soil or *clay*, can be destroyed this way. What is the
point?

13 **fatuous**   pointless; stupid, in an inappropriately cheerful way.

Greater Love

The title refers to Christ's words in the New Testament, quoted by Owen in a letter to his mother in May 1917:

> Christ is literally in no man's land. There men often hear
> His voice: Greater Love hath no man than this, that a man lay
> down his life – for a friend.
> Is it spoken in English only and French?
> I do not believe so.
>
> **(Letter 512, ?16 May 1917, *SL*, page 513)**

(See also *At a Calvary near the Ancre* on page 26.)

The poem is addressed as if to a woman by a romantic lover, but its purpose is to belittle romantic love in comparison to the kind of love shown by soldiers who die for their countrymen, or for their friends. The idealization of soldiers' love and sacrifice and the sensual language of *Greater Love* has given it popularity.

It parodies a romantic poem by the aesthetic poet Algernon Swinburne, *Before the Mirror*:

> White rose in red rose-garden
>   Is not so white;
> Snowdrops that plead for pardon
>   And pine for fright
> Because the hard East blows
> Over their maiden rows
>   Grow not as this face grows from pale to bright.

   7 **slender attitude**   suggests a woman striking a pose in order to attract; also, perhaps, the weakness of the attitude of those who are patriotic about the war.
   9 **rolling**   The writhing of dying soldiers is presented in language that suggests the sexual movements of lovers.
   10 In this poem we see how Owen separates Christ, who shares in

the suffering of the soldiers, from 'God the Father', the warlike Old Testament God, who doesn't care.

22–3 **trail**   In military jargon, to 'trail arms' meant to carry a rifle with the muzzle pointing forwards and the butt near the ground. This is also an ironic reference to the crucifixion. The soldiers are identified with Christ, sacrificed for the sins of mankind, trailing *Your cross* – the weapons they carry for us all – into battle.

24 A reference to Christ's words to Mary Magdalene after the Resurrection. She weeps, not understanding the significance of what has happened and he says, 'Touch me not, for I am not yet ascended to my Father' (John 20:15–17). Owen addresses all those who do not understand the significance of the sacrifice of so many young men.

The Last Laugh

The title underlines the bitterness of this poem, which shows how the war makes an utter mockery of everything soldiers may hold dear. Whether they call on religion, family or love, as they die, the weapons always have 'the last laugh'. Notice the range of words used to depict the laughter of the weapons, personified like a series of grotesque monsters from a child's book of fairy tales. The soldier is made to look like an innocent, *childlike* fool.

1–2 Owen sent an early draft of the poem in a letter to his mother on 18 February 1918, with the comment, 'There is a point where prayer is indistinguishable from blasphemy. There is also a point where blasphemy is indistinguishable from prayer' (Letter 592, *SL*, page 314).

11–12 Notice the similarly sensual language in *Greater Love* on page 36.

Mental Cases

Drawing on what he saw and experienced in Craiglockhart War Hospital, and on his reading of Dante's poetic vision of Hell, *L'Inferno*, Owen paints a distressing picture of those driven to madness by horrific suffering in the trenches. The poem's question-and-answer structure is an ironic parallel to verses from the Book of Revelation in the King James Version of the Bible, which offer a vision of souls in Heaven. These begin, 'What are these which are arrayed in white robes?... These are they which came out of great tribulation... Therefore are they before the throne of God' (Mark Sinfield, quoted in Stallworthy, *The Poems of Wilfred Owen*, page 147).

2 **purgatorial**   According to Roman Catholic belief, Purgatory is an intermediate state in which souls are purified of their sins before proceeding to Heaven, but here it suggests an ongoing state of torment.

2–8 The images echo Dante – and sound somewhat like the medieval view of Hell portrayed in the paintings of Hieronymus Bosch.

6 **fretted sockets**   Their eyes have deep hollows round them, as if from anxiety and insomnia. The question is answered in stanza 3.

13 **sloughs**   mud-filled marshes; it also suggests dead tissue or skin that comes away from the body. Perhaps, too, an allusion to 'the Slough of Despond', which symbolizes a state of deep depression in John Bunyan's *The Pilgrim's Progress*.

15 Victims of trauma, like these shell-shocked soldiers, endlessly relive their horrific experiences in nightmares and flashbacks.

18 **Rucked**   heaped.

23–4 The facial expressions of the mad are grotesque, fixed grins.

26 **rope-knouts... scourging**   A scourge was a knotted whip used as an instrument of divine punishment, as penance for sins.

The Chances

The night before a battle, five soldiers discuss their chances of survival. The most experienced of them, Jimmy, lists five possibilities. Each of the men suffers a different fate. Owen effectively recreates the blunt colloquial style of the 'ordinary' working-class soldier, without being at all patronizing. The poem has clearly been influenced by Siegfried Sassoon's *They* (see Interpretations page 132), which explores a similar theme though without quite the same direct impact that Owen achieves here. It was drafted at Craiglockhart, soon after Owen met Sassoon in August 1917, and revised the following year.

1 **show**   battle (soldiers' slang).
5 **knocked out**   killed.
  cushy   easy; i.e. not a serious wound.
6 **scuppered**   usually 'killed' (soldiers' slang, as in the sinking of a ship), but here, according to the logic of the poem, it means 'taken prisoner'.
  mushy   emotionally upset; nervous.
7 **chops**   pieces; small portions of meat.
8 **props**   legs.
10 **Fritz**   the Germans (soldiers' slang). One of them has been *scuppered*, or taken prisoner.
12 **blighty**   a *cushy* wound, but serious enough for him to be sent home to 'Blighty' (Britain, in soldiers' slang).

The Send-Off

With echoes of the imagery and subdued atmosphere in the sestet of *Anthem for Doomed Youth*, Owen describes a trainload of newly conscripted men setting off for the Front. There are hints that they may well be 'doomed' too. Women have lavishly decorated them with flowers, but these are white, like the flowers traditionally laid on a corpse at a funeral. There is an eerie sense that there is something underhand about their departure – they are like *wrongs hushed-up* – and they seem to vanish into the unknown. The poem was written during April–July 1918.

The Parable of the Old Man and the Young

An ironic take on the Old Testament story of Abraham and his young son Isaac. Abraham is an old man when his beloved son is born. God sets him a severe test of faith, requiring him to offer his son as a sacrifice. Reluctantly, Abraham agrees and makes preparations for the ceremony. Seeing that he is willing to do even this, at the last moment God offers him a way out: he may sacrifice a ram instead, and save his son's life. Owen's poem follows the text from the Book of Genesis very closely for the first 14 lines, but by referring to *parapets and trenches*, he drops in a clue that this is a parable – a story with a parallel or symbolic meaning. In the final couplet he subverts the story completely. Abraham accepts God's reprieve, but here the *old man* does not listen, and pig-headedly goes ahead and kills his son. The 'Old Men' of Europe are those in power, who had the chance to end the war through diplomacy, but chose not to because it would have meant backing down and sacrificing their *Pride*. Instead, as the war continued, they opted to send countless more young men to their deaths.

See Interpretations, page 118.

1 **clave** split.
3 **sojourned** passed time.
8 **parapets** banks or walls, intended to protect soldiers.
16 **seed** offspring; descendants; i.e. the youth and future of Europe. 'Abraham and his seed' were to become the founders of the Israelite tribe.

one by one   adds a sinister emphasis, as if the killing was premeditated or even sadistically enjoyed by the *old man*. It reminds us also that every one of the young men was an individual.

Disabled

This is a compassionate portrait of a terribly disabled young soldier, left sitting in his wheelchair while life goes on around him. A character rather different from Owen, he had been a keen, good-looking footballer, and much fancied by the girls. He had joined the army – one of the Scottish regiments – without having any understanding of the real implications of doing so. He had been flattered into believing that if he wore the kilt, he would be even more attractive. Now, though, he is horribly mutilated, and the girls look away, embarrassed. Formerly fit and virile he is now utterly dependent on others. He takes what little pity and charity he can get, waiting helplessly in the cold for the nurses to come and put him to bed.

Owen drafted the poem at Craiglockhart in October 1917. Both Siegfried Sassoon and Robert Graves thought highly of it.

How would you describe the tone or atmosphere of the poem? What does Owen's use of full rhyme and pentameter rhythm contribute to this?

2   **ghastly suit of grey**   ugly hospital uniform, or cheap civilian suit – very different from his colourful regimental tartan.

7   **Town**   This is likely to be Edinburgh. Owen was familiar with the city during his time at Craiglockhart.

8   Perhaps suggesting the gas-lamps being lit among the trees in the blue light of dusk, possibly in Princes Street Gardens, in the centre of Edinburgh.

14–15   Not only did the girls fancy him, but he was so handsome that an artist had been desperate to paint his portrait.

19 It was as if while he lay bleeding from his wound, he aged rapidly – it put years on him.

20 The spurting blood perhaps suggests ironically the sexual ejaculation no longer possible for him.

21–3 He was a hero of his football team, and saw a smear of blood on his leg as a badge of his virility and prowess.

23 **peg** a drink, probably of whisky or brandy; he was flattered into joining up when he was a little drunk.

25 **kilts** He joined a Scottish regiment, and would have worn the full Highland dress, of the kilt in the regimental tartan, with his skean-dhu, or dagger, tucked into his matching socks.

27 **giddy jilts** flirtatious, capricious young women.

29 **lie** He pretended to be over 18, in order to be accepted for military service.

32–3 See note to line 25.

35 ***Esprit de corps*** team spirit; perhaps he imagined it to be like that of his football team.

38–9 The only person who shows interest is a parson or chaplain doing his charitable duty.

45–6 Now completely dependent, he helplessly waits for nurses to come and put him to bed.

À Terre

In this dramatic monologue, a fatally wounded soldier explores his thoughts about life and his own imminent death. His words are addressed to a poet, who is to record his story in verse. The man desperately wants to live – *one year*, even *One Spring* – and any form of life will do. To be his servant's servant (28), do the dirtiest jobs, or even to survive as a rat in the trenches would be better than this. Later he becomes more resigned to the idea that in dying, he will return to the earth: *I shall be better off with plants*. It will be more peaceful.

The title means 'To Earth', referring to words from the Old Testament (Genesis 3:19) which are echoed in the Burial Service, '... dust thou art, and unto dust shalt thou return'.

The poem was begun at Scarborough in December 1917, and completed in July 1918.

1 **three parts shell**   Many fragments of exploded shells are embedded in the man's body.

5 **peg out soldierly**   die bravely (soldiers' slang).

7–8 **pennies... medals**   Coins used to be placed on the eyelids of the dead to keep their eyes closed. His medals might as well be used for the same purpose. They have led to his death.

9–10 Similarly with the ribbons he's been awarded for bravery. He points out to the poet that he's deliberately using colourful metaphors, suitable for the poem he will write.

13–14 In his poem *Base Details*, Siegfried Sassoon presents a stereotypical, much-disliked Major: *fierce and bald and short of breath/... with my puffy petulant face*, who does not fight but will die safely *in bed*. Even being this would be better than dying.

23–4 He has lost his legs, but believes just feeling the spring wind would enable him to grow new ones.

27 **mummy-case**   His body feels inert, like the solid case of an Egyptian mummy, and he is trapped inside wrapped up in bandages, like a corpse embalmed for burial.

34 **sweep**   chimney sweep.

35 **muckman**   dustman.

37–9 Rats were prevalent in the trenches.

44–7 The officer quotes from Shelley's *Adonais*, in which he mourns the death of Keats:

He is made one with Nature...
He is a presence to be felt and known
In darkness and in light, from herb and stone.

(370–374)

Then he sardonically points out that the ordinary soldiers – even the *dullest* – share the same philosophy: that when they die they will be *Pushing up daisies*.

48–9 The officer makes fun of a commonly believed piece of British propaganda, which suggested that the Germans boiled up dead soldiers to make soap, suggesting they might make soup instead.

52–7 He is now resigned to his death.

59 **fronds** leaves, usually of ferns.

61–3 He thinks his friends will grieve a little, but will soon forget him.

64–5 He asks to have support while he is dying, but once he is dead, his spirit will be *weaned* from needing his body and blood, like a baby that no longer needs its mother's milk.

Exposure

On 4 February 1917, Owen wrote descriptively of his platoon's manoeuvres in icy weather (see Letter 482 on page 58). Later, on 6 April, he wrote that 'We stuck to our line 4 days (and 4 nights) without relief, in the open, and in the snow' (Letter 503, *SL*, page 235). The terrible tension of being trapped in a state of enforced inactivity, exposed to the elements and simultaneously to constant uncertainty and fear of possible attack and sudden death, is powerfully and brilliantly evoked in *Exposure*. The poem, originally titled 'Nothing Happens', charts one cycle of night, through day and back to night, in which the soldiers can do little but wait.

Here we see Owen at the height of his powers, using para-rhyme and aural imagery with the assurance of a musical virtuoso. Look carefully at the sheer variety of sound effects – alliteration, assonance, and internal rhyme – built into almost every line. Consider also the pace of the poem, and the cumulative effect created by the short lines at the ends of each stanza.

1 Owen ironically echoes the opening of Keats's *Ode to a Nightingale*: 'My heart aches, and a drowsy numbness pains/My sense…'

3 **salient** a place where the Front line jutted into enemy territory, where fighting would be fierce and defence particularly important.

14 **grey** German uniforms were grey, and the Germans approached from the East. However, the grey clouds, bringing snow and rain, seem even more threatening to life and morale than the enemy.

23–5 **drowse** Perhaps another echo of Keats (see note to line 1). The soldiers, lying in the snow, dream of life at home in an idealized English countryside of blossom and blackbirds, and seem to be falling into the dangerously drowsy state of hypothermia.

26–30 Compare the words of the popular song, 'Keep the home fires burning... Though your lads are far away, they dream of home', but dreaming of home brings no comfort. This stanza suggests that if the men did return to their homes, they would find them abandoned, and that the doors would be closed against them. The repetition emphasizes the feeling that they have been shut out; they have been sent to the Front and are expected to stay there. Reluctantly they *turn back* to reality.

31–5 The soldiers have to try to hold on to the belief that they are fighting for something worthwhile. They suffer willingly, in order to preserve *kind fires* and truth and freedom for their children. Like Christ, they feel they were born to be sacrificed for others.

34 **loath** unwilling; reluctant.

35 *Either* their suffering is so great because God no longer loves them, *or* the inhumanity of the war shows that humans have ceased to love God.

36–40 Notice the devastating effect of this final stanza. The eyes of both living and dead are *ice*.

The Sentry

In a letter to his mother on 16 January 1917, soon after his arrival in France, Owen describes the incident that inspired this poem (Letter 480 on pages 54–6). While he was in charge of men in a flooded dugout, under heavy bombardment, one of the sentries was blown down and blinded. 'Those fifty hours were the agony of my happy life', he says. The poem was begun at Craiglockhart and is written in the voice of an officer (or Owen himself) telling a listener of this experience, which he still relives in nightmares, though at the time he just got on with what had to be done. Now he tries *not to remember these things*.

1 **Boche** German (soldiers' slang).
8 **whizz-bangs** small, high-velocity shells. The sound they make as they fly through the air is almost simultaneous with the explosion.
13–14 What is the effect of the rather down-to-earth onomatopoeia in these lines?
16 **ruck** heap; mass.
22–3 Compare this repulsive image with the recurring nightmare in *Dulce et Decorum Est* (page 28).
23–6 Although he is still haunted by the experience, at the time, he just had to get on with fulfilling his duties as an officer.
28 In his letter, it is Owen himself who was tempted to give up: 'I nearly broke down and let myself drown in the water that was now slowly rising over my knees' (page 55).
33 **crumps** explosions (soldiers' slang).
33–6 In the closing lines, the blinded sentry ironically has the illusion, for a moment, that he has regained his sight. However, the lights he now claims to see had gone out long before. Jennifer Breen suggests that 'the rest of the platoon, who are literally in darkness, have also lost their insight into events, as perhaps their warmongering society can be said to have done' (Breen, *Wilfred Owen: Selected Poetry and Prose*, 1988, page 216).

Spring Offensive

Owen's last great poem was begun in the summer of 1918. Manuscripts suggest that it was not fully revised or completed.

Men wait to launch an attack in the spring landscape, apparently soothed by nature. Then they go 'over the top' into battle, which involves a rejection of what is natural. Immediately nature seems to turn against them.

The previous spring, Owen had had his own experience of going over the top, which he described in a letter to his youngest brother Colin:

> The sensations of going over the top are about as exhilarating as those dreams of falling over a precipice, when you see the rocks at the bottom surging up to you. I woke up without being squashed. Some didn't. There was an extraordinary exultation in the act of slowly walking forward, showing ourselves openly. ...
>
> Then we were caught in a Tornado of Shells. The various 'waves' were all broken up and we carried on like a crowd moving off a cricket-field. When I looked back and saw the ground all crawling and wormy with wounded bodies, I felt no horror at all but only an immense exultation at having got through the Barrage.
>
> (Letter 510, 14 May 1917, *SL*, page 243)

8–11 The sound of humming insects with the sleepy warmth of summer acts like an injection of a relaxing painkiller or anaesthetic, but it is not enough to counteract the *Sharp* fear of what is to come.

  11 **imminent** looming; threatening; the 'ridge of grass' is the edge of the parapet they will very soon have to cross, when they go over the top.

14–15 **far valley behind... coming up** This is probably not a realistic account of the soldiers' surroundings, but more a reminiscence of past summer fields at home. The image of buttercups that *blessed with gold their slow boots* recalls an idea Owen had used as a boy, when walking through buttercup fields with his brother, who remembered him saying 'Harold's boots are blessed with gold' (Harold Owen, *Journey from Obscurity*, page 40).

19 **little word** the command to attack.

20 **begird** (archaic) to dress, tightening one's belt, ready for a fight; or to brace oneself for an effort or ordeal.

23–6 It is as if the men can no longer look the sun in the face, like a generous friend they have rejected. Instead they have opted to follow war, which is *Mightier*.

29–32 The moment the men launch the attack, it seems that nature turns against them.

30 **cups** Shells exploding create instant, lethal craters, contrasting with the blessing of the buttercups in line 14; also suggests the chalice or cup used for wine that represents the blood of Christ in the communion service.

33 **high place** a phrase often used to describe an altar on a hilltop, used for sacrifices.

37 This line is more an expression of doubt than of pious faith in God. *Some say*, and may believe this, but in the following lines Owen suggests that those who were there, entered hell and survived, and they cannot bring themselves to agree with this religious platitude.

39 **drave** drove.

Notes on the Letters

Letter 330 to Susan Owen, 5 March 1915

At this point, Owen was living at Mérignac, near Bordeaux, where he was employed as a private tutor. He had hoped that his uncle, Edward Quayle, might invest in a trading venture that would finance him to continue his studies and writing, but he was disappointed. Here he discusses his ambition to become a poet and his difficulty in finding any other work that will satisfy him.

To a modern ear, the style of this letter, with its archaic turns of phrase and elaborate metaphors, seems rather self-consciously literary for a young man writing home to his mother. Certainly, this is no hurried note: as with some of his other letters, this one was drafted and revised before the final version was sent.

1–2 **object... subjects** His recent letters had been written for the sake of staying in touch rather than because he had anything much to write about.

2–3 Owen's brother, Harold, later censored many of the letters, removing pages or obliterating passages that might reflect badly on his family.

10–17 **Defence... potsherds** In an extended metaphor, Owen explains that in the battle of life, he can get nowhere unless he has either knowledge (*Science*) or money (*Capital*).

17 **potsherds** broken pieces of pottery.

19 **1911** He refers here to his decision to take the post of Parish Assistant at Dunsden, which ended traumatically with the breakdown of his religious faith.

26–30 **Of the... flower** In another metaphor, Owen explains that writing is the only thing he really wants to do and, to succeed as a poet, he will need years of study and practice.

40 **birth-certificates**   Presumably he means the talents he was born with.

42 **B.A. Craze**   Earlier he had hoped to get a university degree as an external student.

43–5 **'Reverend' pretension... a Call**   becoming a minister of the church. He does, however, reassure his mother that he is still open to the possibility if ever he feels he has a real vocation.

54 **Macbeth's**   In Shakespeare's play, three witches prophesy that Macbeth will become king. Ambition drives him to achieve this by committing murder. However, for his friend, Banquo, the prophecy is: 'Lesser than Macbeth, and greater... Not so happy, yet much happier' (*Macbeth* I:iii).

59–60 **period... isolation**   He prescribes for himself the traditional training of a Romantic poet. He needs to meet like-minded people, but also to spend time in solitude, for his talents to come to fruition.

64 **My hopes...**   In yet another metaphor, Owen suggests that he needs to 'launch' himself before his enthusiasm and energy run out like an ebbing tide. Here he is echoing a passage from Shakespeare's *Julius Caesar*, IV.iii, in which Brutus speaks of the need for bold action at the moment of crisis:

There is a tide in the affairs of men,
Which taken at the flood, leads on to fortune;
Omitted, all the voyage of their life
Is bound in shallows and in miseries.

68–70 Three things hold him back: *Poverty*, *Timidity* and *Indolence*, or laziness.

72–3 **shackles... levers**   iron rings or chains used to restrain prisoners – and the key required to undo them.

Letter 480 to Susan Owen, 16 January 1917

Owen arrived in France at the end of 1916 and joined the 2nd Battalion, Manchester Regiment, near Beaumont Hamel, on 1 January 1917. In bitterly cold, wet weather, their task was to reconnoitre and gain ground in preparation for the Battle of Arras, which followed in April.

Not surprisingly, given the circumstances, it is very noticeable how much more direct his language is here, and in the following letter, compared with the previous one. All the same, he still chooses his words for effect: the mud becomes *an octopus of sucking clay*; and an ironic dry humour makes itself apparent; for example, in the short sentence *I have been in front of it*, or in his comments about the canary.

    6 **seventh hell**   the opposite of 'seventh heaven', which means a state of the most exalted happiness or bliss. Also, in Dante's *La Divina Commedia*, the seventh ring of hell (L'Inferno) was reserved for the punishment of the violent and destructive.

11–19 **We... waders**   Compare the description in *Dulce et Decorum Est*, pages 28–9.

23–57 **Three... casualty**   This incident provided the material for *The Sentry*, page 47.

   48 **support**   bear; tolerate.

   69 **execrate**   curse; detest.

   70 **distinguished countryman**   David Lloyd George, who had been Minister of War before he became Prime Minister in 1916.

Letter 481 to Susan Owen, 19 January 1917

A few days later, Owen and his platoon were still in the same area, near Beaumont Hamel. Here he struggles to find a sufficiently powerful way to put his experience into words. Not even the worst traditional images of hell he can think of – Sodom and Gomorrah, or the Slough of Despond – come close.

After less than three weeks in France, the anger that would be expressed later in poems begins to surface in comments about politicians and attitudes in Britain.

11 **GAS**   As he explains, this was 'only tear-gas', frightening enough, but not like the deadly gas attack he was to describe later in *Dulce et Decorum Est*, page 28.

33 **Gramophone**   old-style record player. This would have been a wind-up model.

35 **Blighty**   Britain (soldiers' slang).

36 **parvenus**   upstarts; those who have recently risen to power and may not be worthy of it. Lloyd George had become Prime Minister in December 1916.

40 **eternal place of gnashing of teeth**   hell.

41 **Slough of Despond**   In John Bunyan's morality tale *The Pilgrim's Progress* (1678), this is a place of utter despair, which Christian has to pass through on his journey from the City of Destruction. A slough is a marsh or mud-filled hole.

42 **Sodom and Gomorrah**   In the Old Testament, these cities were places of grave evil and sexual depravity. As a punishment, God destroyed them by means of a rain of burning sulphur – 'fire and brimstone from the Lord of Heaven' (Genesis 19:24–5).

43–4 **Babylon the Fallen**   another Old Testament city which had fallen out of favour with God.

49–50 **'Somme Pictures'... Kensington**   Unrealistic photographs were released by the army and put out by the press, and perfect 'model' trenches had been dug in London to reassure civilians about conditions at the Front.

55 **Krupp** The Krupp family owned the huge company that manufactured armaments in Germany during the war.

56 **Chlorina-Phosgena** Chlorine and Phosgene were two forms of poison gas used in the war.

61 **agitate** stir up public protest against the war.

   agitated upset or disturbed.

63 **ague** feverish shivering.

Letter 482 to Susan Owen, 4 February 1917

At the end of January, Owen was sent to the Advanced Horse Transport Depot at Abbeville, for special training in methods of transporting supplies to the Front, but not before he had endured another 'tour' of duty, made even worse than before by the freezing weather. John Bell notes:

> The instruction to report to the Advanced Horse Transport Depot
> there survives. On the back of the message form Wilfred
> pencilled some lines from Rabindranath Tagore's *Gitanjali*,
> beginning: 'When I go from hence let this be my parting word,
> that what I have seen is unsurpassable.'
>
> (Bell, *SL*, page 216)

2 **old Town** Abbeville.

10 **wusser** worse.

9–43 **I have… carrion** The experiences described here are probably the basis for the poem *Exposure*, page 45. The man who froze to death may well be the subject of *Futility*, page 36.

15 **Bosche** German (soldiers' slang).

51 **Helmet** Owen had asked his mother to knit him a woollen sleeping-helmet.

54 **Transports** a pun on the word, which can also mean 'ecstasies' in the phrase 'transports of delight'.

55 **Subs.** the other subalterns.

83–5 **I… immensely** Tom Owen found it much easier to

sympathize with and approve of his son's experience as a soldier than his ambition to become a poet.

88 **Quite 10 years ago**   In 1908, Owen and his father had spent a holiday in this part of France.

90 **Auntie Emma**   His mother had shown some of his letters to her sister, Emma Gunston.

94–5 **extra for me… Ugliness**   Owen suggests that because he is a sensitive poet who has aligned himself with the aesthetic view that beauty is the supreme good, ugliness is particularly hard for him to bear. (See Interpretations, page 124.)

101 **In poetry…**   Earlier war poetry refers to the 'Glorious dead'. In his letters, Owen is finding ways of describing the reality that confronts him, but not, as yet, in poetry.

106 **Quotha?**   (archaic) she says? Distaste is something of an understatement.

107 **Tankerville Street**   in Shrewsbury.

120–3 **The Letter… London**   Owen had tutored the four de la Touche boys, at Mérignac in 1915. They were now at school in Lancashire. Their aunt ran a hospital for Belgian refugees.

Letter 664 to Siegfried Sassoon, 10 October 1918

Owen returned to the Front at the end of August 1918. At the beginning of October he was involved in the attack on the Hindenburg Line, near Joncourt. As they tried to take cover, his servant – and perhaps friend – Private Jones, was shot through the head.

5 **O.C. D Coy**   Officer in Charge of D Company.

6–7 **sheer… eipthet**   He can't think of an adjective powerful enough to describe the experience.

10 ***Counter-Attack***   Sassoon's latest collection of poetry, which had recently been published.

16–18 **My senses are charred. I shall feel again**   It is as if he remembers what he had written in *Insensibility*: that to numb the feelings may be necessary for survival.

20 **Deceased**   As an officer, Owen has to send the letters of dead soldiers back to their relatives, but he also intends that one day he will write of their deaths in his books.

22 **M.C.**   Owen was recommended for the Military Cross for 'conspicuous gallantry and devotion to duty in the attack on the Fonsomme Line on 1st/2nd October 1918'.

26–7 **peace talk… *'en pamoisons'***   (See also line 47 below.) Enclosed with this letter was a 'Special Order of the Day from the 4th Army Commander' which he was expected to proclaim to his men:

'Peace Talk in any form is to cease in Fourth Army.'
'All ranks are warned against the disturbing influence of dangerous peace talk.'

Owen is joking about this with Sassoon, suggesting it would have caused him to 'swoon'.

36 **wrens**   Sassoon wrote later:

I had described how, early one morning, a golden-crested wren had appeared in my bedroom and perched on my pillow, thereby affording me the innocent pleasure of releasing it at the open window. Reading his rejoinder to this almost maiden-auntlike piece of news, I probably told myself that war experience was mainly composed of acute contrasts, of which this – in conjunction with his – seemed a classic example.

(Sassoon, *Siegfried's Journey*, page 73)

39 **exposed flanks**   He doesn't want to be exposed to bullets or shellfire – but Owen probably also intended a sexual innuendo.

45 **Tamboo**   shelter.

47 **the choicest of specimens**   Owen is being sarcastic about the 'Special Order'; see lines 26–7 above.

Letter 673 to Susan Owen, 31 October 1918

This is the last surviving letter from Owen to his mother. He was killed a few days later, on 4 November, leading his platoon in an attack on the Sambre–Oise Canal. The war ended one week later. Owen often wrote reassuringly to his mother, but with the benefit of hindsight, it is hard not to feel that there is something prophetic about the tone of resigned cheerfulness here.

32–3 **it will be well over** The attack was planned for early morning on 4 November, 3 days later.

Interpretations

Themes

Owen came into his own as a poet when he embraced the war as the focus of his work. He had been training himself to write since he was a teenager, mimicking Keats and other poets and, in the process, exploring a variety of fairly conventional poetic themes – love, nature and death, for example. He had always written about his own experiences and his inner world, in his letters if not always in his poetry. However, it was when he met Siegfried Sassoon and came to believe that writing realistically about the war was not only valid but necessary, that his particular combination of personality, experience and talent came to fruition. He had found a subject that he could be passionate about.

During 1918, he was putting together a collection of poems for a book and started to write the Preface for this. You will find a draft of his Preface on page 19.

Activity

Read the Preface on page 19.

Compare the Preface with these paragraphs from the Introduction to a popular anthology of *Songs and Sonnets for England in Wartime*, published in 1914.

> … In the stress of a nation's peril some of its greatest songs are born. In the stress of a nation's peril the poet at last comes into his own again, and with clarion call he rouses the sleeping soul of the empire. Prophet, he is, champion and consoler…

> … What can so nobly uplift the hearts of a people facing war with its unspeakable agony as music and poetry? The sound of martial music steels men's hearts before battle. The sound of martial words inspires human souls to do and to endure. God, his poetry, and His music are the Holy Trinity of war.

> (quoted in Hibberd, *Poetry of the First World War*, page 31)

Discuss or make notes on what Owen has to say about the purpose of his work, commenting on ways in which it differs from the views expressed in the quotation above.

Discussion

First of all, Owen makes it clear that he is *not* writing the sort of war poetry that conventionally had been expected, especially in the earlier years of the war. The traditional subjects for war poets – glory, honour, might, and majesty – are abstract ideas. Owen, however, writes simply about 'War, and the pity of War' – the real experience of it and what it does to people.

The role of the traditional war poet is to stir up nationalistic feeling, to encourage or champion the troops of one side, and to console those who suffer or lose loved ones by presenting war as a noble cause. Owen, on the other hand, says he is deliberately choosing not to name people or places, so that his words about war will be relevant to people of other nations and future generations. He also states plainly that his 'elegies' (poems of mourning) do not – or perhaps *cannot* – offer any consolation to the generation who have suffered, though they may do so to people in the future.

Owen shows his respect and compassion for the soldiers of the war – the real heroes – when he says 'English Poetry is not yet fit to speak of them'. It is as if he doesn't believe any poet living could do justice to their suffering.

The writer of the Introduction refers to the war in old-fashioned religious terms, as if it is a sort of crusade supported by God. Owen uses no religious language here, though in some poems and letters he explores contrasting religious attitudes to the war.

Overall, the Introduction is written in elevated language and a rhetorical style, as if the author is making a speech at us: for example, in the repeated opening phrase of the first two sentences, or the grouping of ideas in threes in 'Prophet, he is, champion and consoler'. Archaic vocabulary, such as 'peril' or 'clarion call' (the language of medieval chivalry), and abstract ideas like 'honour' and 'glory', make this writing remote from real experience.

Owen's language here is very plain and simple. He claims he is 'not concerned with Poetry', by which we can understand that he was more concerned with what he was saying than with writing 'poetically' or producing the sort of work the writer of the Introduction quoted above considered to be 'Poetry'. His aim is to be true to experience, and in doing so, to be a 'true Poet'. 'The Poetry is in the pity': *real* poetry comes from the expression of genuine feeling, not from fancy language or high-flown ideas. His purpose is to do the only thing a poet *can* do: to 'warn' humanity of the consequences of war.

'The pity of War'

Owen confronts us with the pity of war in many different forms. He explores war's destructiveness, its threat to civilization and its values, its impact on nature and, above all, its devastating effect on human life and spirit.

His most wide-reaching expression of this occurs in *Strange Meeting* (page 32). In a mythical, dreamlike hell, a dead soldier encounters *the enemy [he] killed* (40). Through their dialogue, Owen explores *The pity of war* (25) on both a personal and a universal level. On one hand, we see the tragedy of individuals, of young men who share similar hopes and ideals forced to kill each other: ... *Whatever hope is yours/Was my life also* (16–17).

At the same time, the poem warns of war's deleterious effect on human civilization as a whole. In the early twentieth century, people generally still believed in 'progress', trusting that human development was perpetually in a positive direction. *Strange Meeting* is an expression of despair: these two young men, 'true poets', perhaps, wanted to reveal *the truth* about war, but the truth *must die now* and will remain *untold* (24). No lessons will be learned from the war; nobody will *break ranks* and challenge the conventional view; and nations will not move forward, but instead *trek [away] from progress* (29) . Sadly, the history of the last 90 years suggests that Owen was not only a 'true' poet, but a prophet.

Nature

Nature features frequently in poetry of the First World War, particularly when it throws into relief the devastation, inhumanity and *un*naturalness of war. Sassoon, like many others, drew contrasts between blighted landscapes and the plants and flowers that managed to survive. On the first day of the Battle of the Somme, he was struck by the terrible incongruity of the slaughter under a glorious blue sky and while larks were singing overhead. Similarly, in Owen's Letter 664 to Sassoon on 10 October 1918 (page 62), he describes how he 'found brave companionship in a poppy, behind whose stalk I took cover from five machine-guns and several howitzers'. In Sassoon's response, included in the notes on page 107, he comments that 'war experience was mainly composed of acute contrasts'.

Owen does not usually draw such blatant contrasts; rather, nature and its destruction become absorbed into the theme of much of his poetry – the pity of war.

The devastated Somme battleground

Activity

Look at Letter 480 on pages 54–6 and Letter 482 on pages 58–62. Look also at the poem *The Show* on page 34. Discuss or make notes on how Owen portrays landscape and nature in these texts.

Discussion

In Letter 480, Owen uses the most extreme images of hell and disease in an attempt to describe a landscape in which nature has no part. These images of sickness are reworked to create the ghastly *sad land* he depicts in *The Show*. In Letter 482, the landscapes are 'hideous' and nature is described in terms of absence ('Not a blade of grass, not an insect') or of threat. For example, the wind is 'deadly' and 'the shadow of a big hawk, scenting carrion' hovers overhead.

War is unnatural. It constitutes an attack on nature and, in return, nature becomes hostile to those involved in it. In *Spring Offensive* (page 48), soldiers waiting to attack are soothed by the natural beauty and warmth of a fine, early summer day. Nature has the power to heal, or at least to anaesthetize their anguish, *Like an injected drug for their bodies' pains* (10). But when they are ordered to go 'over the top', it is as if they have ungratefully rejected *The sun, like a friend with whom their love is done* (24) and allied themselves with war in an offensive against nature. As the enemy opens fire, it seems that nature immediately retaliates too:

> ... instantly the whole sky burned
> With fury against them; earth set sudden cups
> In thousands for their blood
>
> (*Spring Offensive*, 29–31)

Making nature threatening or hostile, or equating it with the enemy, occurs also in *Exposure* (page 45), where men are forced to wait endlessly for something to happen, in freezing conditions that are ultimately more hazardous than the *Sudden successive flights of bullets* (16). The cold weather front that moves in, with the dawn, from the east, in *ranks on shivering ranks* (14) of grey

113

clouds, blends with the threat from ranks of enemy troops in their grey uniforms. Even the pleasant, *grassier* images of nature are a dangerous trap. As the men become drowsy and daydream of blossoms and blackbirds (24), they risk hypothermia and freezing to death.

A poem in which nature is viewed rather differently is *À Terre* (page 43), in which a dying soldier, desperate to live on almost any terms finally resigns himself to '*Pushing up daisies*' (47).

Activity

Read *À Terre*, paying particular attention to lines 44–57. How does the soldier resign himself to death?

Discussion

The soldier embraces the idea of becoming *one with nature* (44), of being absorbed back into the earth and so helping to fertilize the next round in the cycle of death and regeneration. This is one form in which life could continue, however minimally. The reference to Shelley (see Notes on the Poems, page 95) is ironical. Although the soldier imagines that he will be *better off with plants that share/ More peaceably the meadow and the shower*, this is hardly going to be the sort of Romantic immortality envisaged by Shelley.

Doomed youth

Owen's most poignant and most powerful expressions of *the pity of War* are reserved for its human victims. Whether he writes of death en masse or of the suffering of individuals, the terrible waste of life, youth, beauty and potential moved him to write with sorrow, anger and bitterness. From his initial rather dismissive view of ordinary soldiers, whom he once described as 'expressionless lumps' (Letter 476, SL, page 208), he came to feel a deep compassion for them. Dominic Hibberd suggests that homosexual feelings may have intensified Owen's love for the men.

With Sassoon's help, Wilfred was able to deal with the most difficult problem of all in the process of integrating himself with the world he lived in. His sexuality could be central to his writing, without ever being visible to people who might disapprove of it. His poetry, like his friend's, would be driven by love for men, an entirely honourable motive that could be openly stated yet at the same time kept hidden.

(Hibberd, *Wilfred Owen: A New Biography*, page 346)

His first encounters with death are recorded in Letters 481 and 482 (pages 56–62) where he is repelled first by the smell and then by the sight of 'the distortion of the dead, whose unburiable bodies sit outside the dug-outs all day, all night, the most execrable sights on earth'.

Death on a vast, impersonal scale is the subject of *Anthem for Doomed Youth* (page 22). The young soldiers go to war innocent and unthinking, *as cattle* (1) to the slaughter. Their deaths are unceremonious and undignified. They are mourned only at a distance, where their families draw down the blinds and grieve.

Other poems focus more closely on the deaths of specific men, though usually 'no localising background is given, no attempt made to individualise' them. As a result, they 'become universalised'. Like 'the Unknown Warrior' commemorated at Westminster Abbey, they come to represent many men (Welland, *Wilfred Owen: A Critical Study*, page 75).

Activity

Read *The Last Laugh* (page 37) and *Futility* (page 36). Compare the way the deaths of individuals are presented in these poems.

Discussion

The Last Laugh shows the dying moments of three representative soldiers. Each of them calls on one of the things that soldiers rely on for comfort and support: religion, family and love. Their words make us aware of the personal reality behind each death and the images of the dying men are poignant – one has a *childlike* (7) smile. In *Futility*, soldiers discover the body of a dead companion who has died in the night. They

Move him into the sun (1), hoping that its warmth will *rouse him* (6). Again, we are reminded of the man's personal reality, of what has been lost. The *fields half-sown* (3) may represent other unfulfilled hopes and ventures as well as the soldier's former life as a farmer.

The poems create different feelings. *The Last Laugh* may at first appear almost light-hearted, but becomes sinister as we recognize the terrifying, impersonal destructiveness of the weapons. *Futility* is much more obviously sombre and deeply sad.

Both poems suggest bitterly that death in war makes a mockery of life. In *The Last Laugh* the armaments are personified as sinister comic caricatures, which *guffawed... tittered... hooted and groaned* with laughter, showing their utter disregard for the soldiers and all they hold dear. *Futility* ends with a cry of absolute despair. Death in war mocks the sheer energy and effort that has gone into creating a human being, from the first appearance of life on a *cold star* (9) to a mother's nurturing of her son's body, *so dear achieved* (10). It all seems *fatuous* (13), like a sick, pointless joke.

Perhaps, though, the dead are not in the end the most pitiable victims of war. Death, at least, is final, and suffering is ended. In *The Next War*, a poem not included here, Owen has a soldier say, *Death was never enemy of ours*. The dead cannot be *roused*. They become remote, and even, sometimes, strangely beautiful, as Owen depicts in *I Saw His Round Mouth's Crimson* (page 24).

Part of telling the truth about war involves exposing the *wrongs hushed up* and making people see what they would rather not see. Some victims cannot be transformed into glorious dead heroes, but live on, an awkward reminder of the real nature of war: the wounded and the mad.

Activity

Now read *Disabled* (page 41).
- How does Owen present the young man's life before the war, compared to how it is now?
- What does he reveal about the young man's motives for joining up?
- How do the people around respond to this victim of the war?

Discussion

- In the past, he was a typical, lively boy. He was sporty, a footballer who enjoyed a drink with the lads and flirting with the girls. He was so good-looking that there was *an artist silly for his face* (14). His life was full of light and colour. He enjoyed the *swing* (7) of town. Now, he is severely disabled and sits helplessly in his wheelchair. His life is dark, cold and colourless like the *ghastly suit of grey* (2) he is forced to wear. Even the sound of children playing near him is *saddening* and sombre *like a hymn* (4). He seemed to have everything to live for, but now all his future holds is *a few sick years in institutes* (40), dependent on others for *whatever pity they may dole* (42).
- When he joined up it was out of vanity as much as anything else. Someone suggested *he'd look a god in kilts* (25) – the traditional uniform of soldiers in Scottish regiments. He thought it would impress the girls. He was excited after a football game and a little drunk, too.
- He used to be treated like a hero when he'd scored in a football match, but now, when he supposedly *is* a hero, nobody wants to know. Any girls who see him immediately look away *to the strong men that were whole* (44). Probably the only women he comes into contact with now are nurses and even they *touch him like some queer disease* (13). He is dependent on them for everything, but they leave him out in the cold in more ways than one. No one seems aware of his suffering.

In *Insensibility* (page 30) Owen explores the value of dissociation, the psycho-physical mechanism which enables humans to survive trauma by shutting down access to their feelings. He describes men who are *Happy* (19) in that *Having seen all things red* (23), they no longer respond to shocking experiences. In *Mental Cases* (page 38), however, he describes those for whom this mechanism can no longer offer protection. They go mad or become the victims of shell-shock. Overwhelmed by horror, they are like souls in Purgatory, condemned to exist perpetually in a state that is neither life nor death, endlessly reliving the unspeakable things they have seen and known. These men are hidden away in the *twilight* (1) of a hospital, but Owen takes the reader there and uncompromisingly exposes their agony:

> Always they must see these things and hear them...
> Therefore still their eyeballs shrink tormented
> Back into their brains, because on their sense
> Sunlight seems a blood-smear; night comes blood-black
>
> (15, 19–21)

They reach out to *us who dealt them war and madness* (28), but Owen offers no hope that their plight will be heeded.

Religion and war

As a boy, Owen was immersed in the evangelical form of Christianity to which his mother was devoted, but during his time as Parish Assistant to the Reverend Henry Wigan at Dunsden, in Oxfordshire, he began to have doubts. His duties there included visiting poor and sick parishioners. For the first time he encountered real deprivation and began to feel the compassion for suffering humanity that was later to infuse his war poetry. Moreover, the literature he was reading led him to question the rather simplistic belief system he was required to espouse, and offered world views that were much more compatible with his inner experience.

Amid the fervour of a Parish Revival, he became so distressed by his inner conflict that he wrote that his nerves were 'in a shocking state... Just as if one had been over-long in a putrid atmosphere and had got to the advanced stage of being painfully conscious of it' (Letter 168, *SL*, page 67). Poetry was his solace, as he explains in *On My Songs* (page 23), but it was clear that he would have to give it up if he were to continue working for the Church. This was a choice he was not prepared to make.

However, as with many other First World War writers, his Christian upbringing was too strongly woven into the fabric of his being to be eradicated. The religious texts he knew well provided a rich source of vocabulary and imagery. Old

Testament images abound in his attempts to describe his first experiences at the Front. No Man's Land is 'like the eternal place of gnashing of teeth… the fires of Sodom and Gomorrah could not light a candle to it – to find the way to Babylon the Fallen' (Letter 481, page 57). The idea of soldiers being sacrificed for the benefit of others often led to them being seen as Christlike, and Owen, like other poets, used this idea on several occasions: for example, *Greater Love* (page 36) and *At a Calvary near the Ancre* (page 26).

In his later work, it becomes apparent that he has never let go of a fundamental sympathy with the basic values of Christ's teachings. What has happened is that this has become separated both from the Old Testament view of a warlike, vengeful Father-God and from the formalized religion of the Churches, whose ministers openly supported the war.

Activity

Read the following short poem:

Soldier's Dream

I dreamed kind Jesus fouled the big-gun gears;
And caused a permanent stoppage in all bolts;
And buckled with a smile Mausers and Colts;
And rusted every bayonet with His tears.

And there were no more bombs, of ours or Theirs,
Not even an old flint-lock, nor even a pikel.
But God was vexed, and gave the power to Michael;
And when I woke he'd seen to our repairs.

(Stallworthy, ed., *Wilfred Owen: The Complete Poems and Fragments*, page 358)

What view of God does it present?

Discussion

Here we can see clearly the separation between God the Father and God the Son. *Kind Jesus* tries to bring the war to a standstill, by putting out of action all the armaments of both sides, but he is overruled by his Father, God, who sends in the warlike Archangel Michael to repair them all in order that the war can continue. Christ is compassionate, but the conservative and traditional God supports the war.

Another poem in which Owen draws on religious material to make a related point is *The Parable of the Old Man and the Young* (page 40). In his retelling of the Old Testament story of Abraham and Isaac, the old man demonstrates his obedience to God by preparing to offer his son as a sacrifice. In the original version, God recognizes his devotion and at the last moment grants Abraham a reprieve – he can kill a ram instead. In Owen's version, however, the old man refuses to listen and kills his son, illustrating the view that the 'Old Men' – the political leaders of Europe – could have ended the war much more quickly if they had been prepared to sacrifice their pride and negotiate a peace settlement. Instead, they chose to prolong the war, sending countless young men to their deaths. This was the view Sassoon had expressed in his famous public statement (see Owen in Context, page 13).

Activity

Now read *At a Calvary near the Ancre* (page 26) and the notes on pages 76–7, along with this passage from a letter written in May 1917:

> ... I am more and more Christian as I walk the unchristian ways of Christendom. Already I have comprehended a light which never will filter into the dogma of any national church: namely that one of Christ's essential commands was: Passivity at any price! Suffer dishonour and disgrace; but never resort to arms. Be bullied, be outraged, be killed; but do not kill. It can only be ignored: and I think pulpit professionals are ignoring it very skilfully and successfully indeed.
>
> (Letter 512, *SL*, pages 246–7)

What is Owen saying about Christian faith and the Church?

Discussion

As he gained more experience of war, Owen became increasingly certain that for a true Christian, pacifism was an absolute requirement, and that 'pure Christianity will not fit in with pure patriotism' (see also Notes to the Poems, page 76). 'Christendom' – or organized religion and the church hierarchy – had become 'unchristian' by supporting the war and, in so doing, ignoring one of Christ's most important New Testament commandments. Later in Letter 512, Owen says: 'This practice of <u>selective ignorance</u> is, as I have pointed out, one cause of the War. Christians have deliberately <u>cut</u> some of the main teachings of their code'.

Gentle Christ is also *denied* by the priests and scribes in *At a Calvary near the Ancre* (8), who have allied themselves with war and have done so for political reasons: they *bawl allegiance to the state* (10).

It is interesting to notice that propaganda devices such as appropriating God's help for one's own side or using Christian teachings to support political rhetoric are as rife today as ever they were in Owen's time. For example, during the American presidential election in 2008, Republican Vice-Presidential candidate Sarah Palin expressed her conviction that the war in Iraq was God's will. Speaking of the troops being posted to Iraq, including her own son, Track, she declared: 'Our national leaders are sending them out on a task from God'.

Language and style

By the time Owen was writing his last great war poems, he was forging his own distinctive personal style. Various writers and literary traditions had captured his imagination at different stages in his life and all of these are reflected in some way in his work.

Literary influences

Unlike Sassoon, Owen was not educated at a public school and so was less of a classical scholar than many poets. He did not have the same depth of knowledge of Latin and Greek literature to draw on. However, he did have a good grounding in English literature, including the works of Shakespeare, Spenser and Milton. In his boyhood, Victorian poets like Tennyson were the standard popular fare. Owen enjoyed Tennyson's poems and could recite many of them from memory. The Victorians had a taste for the old stories from the tradition of chivalry and courtly love. Tennyson's *Idylls of the King*, which blends Arthurian legends with contemporary ideas, was very popular and Owen would have known it well. *The Charge of the Light Brigade*, still popular today, is a perfect example of the kind of 'clarion call' that people expected to find in poetry about war at the beginning of the twentieth century.

In his earliest work, Owen tends to use quite a lot of rather archaic, 'literary' language, as if he believed that this was what was expected in poetry, and some of his titles and subjects clearly echo Tennyson. A poem of Tennyson's is entitled *Supposed Confessions of a Secondrate Sensitive Mind*; Owen wrote the *Supposed Confessions of a Secondrate Sensitive Mind in Dejection*:

> Time was when I have loved the bards whose strains
> Saddened the heart, and wrought a heavy mood;
> Aye, and my spirit felt a joy to brood
> O'er melodies which told of ancient pains.

(1–4)

Sometimes this tendency persisted even in his late work. For example, he uses archaic words like *begird* (20) and *drave* (39) in *Spring Offensive*, one of the last poems he worked on. However, other poets and styles Owen encountered later were to have a big impact on his work.

Keats and the Romantics

As a teenager, Owen developed a particular sympathy with the writers of the Romantic era. He responded first to Wordsworth, who had set out new principles for poetry at the end of the eighteenth century which were more in tune with the revolutionary ideals of the time. Challenging the artificial, mannered style that had been popular, Wordsworth declared in his Preface to *Lyrical Ballads* that poetry should be rooted in real experience and feeling, and written in language that was more like 'the real language of men'. Poetry did not have to be about 'special' subjects or famous people, but could feature 'incidents and situations in common life', and nature should be the main source of inspiration. Above all, imagination was important, allowing poets to empathize with others and enabling them to see what is special in ordinary things.

In April 1911, Owen discovered the work of John Keats. Like Wordsworth, Keats believed in being sincere and true to individual experience, but he was different in that he also turned to the 'pastoral' world of Greek and Roman myth as a source of ideas and inspiration for his poetry. Keats suffered from tuberculosis, had watched his beloved brother die from the disease and knew his own life would be short. Keats became Owen's ideal: he felt a deep emotional connection with the young poet who had been so aware of the beauty, transience and fragility of life, though he did not know that, like his hero, he too would die at the age of 25. Holidaying in Devon, he made a pilgrimage to a house where Keats had stayed for a while and recorded his excitement in a sonnet (see page 19). He was also intensely moved when he read biographies of Keats: 'I cannot read... for long without getting wound up. I have more than once turned hot and cold and trembly over the first haemorrhage scene; and sobbed over Severn's "He is gone... "' (Letter 157, *SL*, page 66).

In *On My Songs* (page 23), we can get an idea of how close Owen felt to poets like Keats, who seemed, through their poetry, to offer him understanding. It comforted him to feel that their struggles had been similar to his own.

Many of Owen's early poems are closely modelled on Keats, and even in later war poems there are often echoes of Keats's diction. You can recognize Keats's influence in:

* the prevalence of 'lyrical', descriptive or reflective poems
* the wish to write about genuine personal experience and responses

- the use of rich, sensual vocabulary and description
- references to mythical beings or characters from classical literature, though this becomes rare in his later work.

The notes on individual poems indicate where some specific echoes of Keats and other poets can be found.

Keats's famous *Ode to a Nightingale* was a particular favourite of Owen's. Several of his poems refer to it or conjure a similar atmosphere, though in very different circumstances. See, for example, the activity on the opening stanza of *Exposure* on page 142. If you have not studied Keats's work, read the following extract from his famous ode now to get a flavour of his style. See if you can recognize similarities as you study Owen's poems.

Ode to a Nightingale

My heart aches, and a drowsy numbness pains
    My sense, as though of hemlock I had drunk,
Or emptied some dull opiate to the drains
    One minute past, and Lethe-wards had sunk:
'Tis not through envy of thy happy lot,
    But being too happy in thine happiness –
        That thou, light-wingèd Dryad of the trees,
        In some melodious plot
Of beechen green, and shadows numberless,
    Singest of summer in full-throated ease.

Tailhade: Aesthetes and Decadents

Owen's reading would have included the work of late Romantic writers, including those who belonged to what is called the 'Aesthetic' movement of the late nineteenth century, such as Algernon Charles Swinburne. Their central idea was the pursuit of 'pure beauty'. Writers and artists aimed above all to capture exquisite sensations and images.

Laurent Tailhade belonged to a group who had taken this idea further. They called themselves 'Decadents', and their group included French and poets such as Paul Verlaine and

Charles Baudelaire. To them, art was amoral: issues of good and evil were considered irrelevant. Almost any behaviour was acceptable in the pursuit of beauty, and Decadent art often deliberately aimed to shock the complacent middle classes. The members of the group were often homosexual, or explored sado-masochism, blurring the dividing line between horror and beauty, pain and pleasure. (For example, one poem by Baudelaire describes a rotting carcase in language that makes it sound – in some ways – incredibly beautiful.) Sometimes, they mocked religious traditions; for example, by treating religious sacraments as opportunities for aesthetic effect rather than as spiritual experiences.

Wilfred Owen in uniform in 1916

Activity

Look at *Maundy Thursday* on page 23. To what extent does it reflect the influence of Decadent ideas?

Discussion

Attending the Catholic ceremony of The Veneration of the Cross – which takes place on Good Friday – the narrator describes how various members of the congregation approach to kiss the crucifix, with different degrees of fervour. For Owen, the ceremony seems without meaning: *The Christ was thin, and cold, and very dead* (12). When his turn comes, he opts to kiss the *warm live hand* (14) of the *server-lad* (1), which offers a much more attractive sensation. This would probably be regarded as blasphemous and somewhat shocking to conventionally religious people.

The Decadents also believed civilization had passed its peak and was now in its 'autumn' – ripe and brilliant, but sliding towards decline and decay, as had happened in the last days of ancient Rome. Tailhade linked this idea to the war and Owen clearly refers to it in *1914* – his earliest attempt at a war poem – in which the war is seen in the abstract, as the inevitable winter purging the world for a new spring. (See page 24.)

Elements of the Decadent style are echoed in some of Owen's later work too. In their endeavour to make poetry beautiful and sensual, the Decadent poets used rich imagery and paid attention to the sound qualities of words.

Activity

Consider this comment: 'Themes of passive suffering, and smiling martyrdom consistently recur in Decadent art, pain and death being welcome as supreme sensations' (Hibberd, *Wilfred Owen: A New Biography*, page 171).

Now look at the way soldiers and death are described in *Greater Love* on page 36 and *I Saw His Round Mouth's Crimson* on page 24.

Can you detect any elements of the Decadent approach?

Discussion

In both of these poems, death is described in a way that brings it very close to being beautiful, and also sensual and sexual. The image of a red, bleeding mouth is very typical of Decadent art and writing. The description of soldiers in *Greater Love* appeals to the senses, using colour, shape, sound and texture. Phrases such as *Trembles not exquisite like limbs knife-skewed* (8) or *hearts made great with shot* (20) make the sensation of pain excruciating but also somehow pleasurable, and have a sexual undertone. The poem also explores ideas of sacrifice and martyrdom.

Harold Monro and Georgian poetry

In 1916, Owen was pleased to have the opportunity to meet the poetry enthusiast Harold Monro, who not only ran the specialist Poetry Bookshop in London, and organized readings and discussions, but even provided cheap lodgings for struggling poets. Owen rented a room from him for a while. Back in 1911, while he was working as a Parish Assistant and struggling with the evangelical Christianity he had begun to find repressive, Owen had come across Monro's collection of poems, *Before Dawn*. Monro's ideas were subversive: he was critical of the Church and proposed a 'new society, in which people would be responsible for their own destiny, living close to nature without notions of any supernatural God or paradise. Sexuality would be open and free, and restrictions such as formal marriage would be abolished' (Hibberd, *Wilfred Owen: A New Biography*, page 89). Owen was intrigued and experimented with writing in the plainer, more direct style used by Monro, which was to become known as 'Georgian'.

Monro was also a publisher and, with Edward Marsh, was responsible for the five collections of *Georgian Poetry* published between 1912 and 1922. King George V had come to the throne in 1910 and Marsh invented the term 'Georgian poetry' to define what was then seen as a more modern way of writing which challenged the rather pompous, conventional and moralistic verse of the late Victorian and Edwardian literary establishment. Well-known poets such as John Masefield and Walter de la Mare appear in these anthologies, along with many we never hear of nowadays. Rupert Brooke and Siegfried Sassoon also contributed.

Georgian poetry tends to have a rather bad press these days: it is considered 'twee' and unadventurous compared with the far more daring experiments of Modernist writers such as W.B. Yeats, T.S. Eliot and Ezra Pound. Often the poems are about the English countryside and use simple, traditional verse forms. Paul Fussell suggests that 'a standard way of writing the Georgian poem was to get as many flowers into it as possible' (Fussell, *The Great War and Modern Memory*, page 243).

However, Georgian poetry was widely read and very popular in its day and, particularly in its earlier years, was seen as a refreshing change. Like Wordsworth and the Romantics a century or so earlier, Georgian poetry aimed to stay closer to genuine experience and to use the 'real language of men'. The intention was to make poetry accessible to and readable for ordinary people.

When Monro saw Owen's work, he was very impressed, but thought it rather old-fashioned. He advised him to be less 'Keatsian' and a little more modern. Gradually, Owen began to integrate some of this new approach into his work. Later, working on his poetry at Craiglockhart, he began to concentrate on writing about real life rather than abstract ideas, using much plainer language. His war experiences provided plenty of subject matter. Later, he was to say that he wanted to write in a way that would be readable for the ordinary soldier.

Siegfried Sassoon

Siegfried Sassoon in 1915

The final great influence on Owen's work was his friendship and collaboration with Siegfried Sassoon. At Craiglockhart, Owen read some of Sassoon's realistic and satirical poems and felt that they gave powerful expression to the actual experience of war in a way that he had not encountered before:

> I have just been reading Siegfried Sassoon, and am feeling at a very high pitch of emotion. Nothing like his trench life sketches has ever been written or ever will be written. Shakespeare reads vapid after these. Not of course because Sassoon is a greater artist, but because of the subjects, I mean. I think if I had the choice of making friends with Tennyson or with Sassoon I should go to Sassoon.
>
> That is why I have not yet dared to go up to him and parley in a casual way.
>
> (Letter 540, *SL*, pages 269–70)

Owen overcame his awe and called on Sassoon. Sassoon took an interest in his work, reinforcing the advice he had received from Monro: concentrate on writing about real experience and use plainer language. Owen went on to do this in poems like *Dulce et Decorum Est* and *Disabled*.

Sassoon also showed Owen that war experiences, even the most horrific and painful, could be appropriate subjects for poetry. If they were presented truthfully and with compassion, it was even possible to create something beautiful out of them. Owen was particularly moved by *The Death Bed*, in which Sassoon describes a young soldier dying in hospital.

Activity

Read these extracts from Sassoon's *The Death Bed*.

The Death Bed

(Extract A)

He drowsed and was aware of silence heaped
Round him, unshaken as the steadfast walls;
Aqueous like floating rays of amber light,
Soaring and quivering in the wings of sleep.
Silence and safety; and his mortal shore
Lipped by the inward, moonless waves of death.

Someone was holding water to his mouth.
He swallowed, unresisting; moaned and dropped
Through crimson gloom to darkness; and forgot
The opiate throb and ache that was his wound.

[...]

(Extract B)

Light many lamps and gather round his bed.
Lend him your eyes, warm blood, and will to live.
Speak to him; rouse him; you may save him yet.
He's young; he hated War; how should he die
When cruel old campaigners win safe through?

But death replied: 'I choose him.' So he went,
And there was silence in the summer night;
Silence and safety; and the veils of sleep.
Then, far away, the thudding of the guns.

(Sassoon, The War Poems, pages 52–3, lines 1–10, 34–42)

Now look at Owen's *I Saw His Round Mouth's Crimson* (page 24) and
Futility (page 36).

- What similarities and differences can you find between the
  imagery and mood in *I Saw His Round Mouth's Crimson* and
  extract A?
- In what ways does *Futility* echo extract B? How does Owen's
  attitude to his subject differ from Sassoon's?
- What evidence can you find in these poems that it is possible to
  create beauty out of painful experiences, if they are presented
  truthfully and with compassion?
- You may like to extend your explorations into more of Owen's
  work.

Discussion

- Both poets use images of sunlight giving way to darkness to
  describe the soldiers' lapsing into death or unconsciousness; they
  use the same 'colour scheme' too – Sassoon has *crimson gloom*
  while Owen sees the *crimson deepen* like the end of a sunset
  (1–2); both have a 'large-scale' feel, referring to skies and seas.
  Sassoon's poem seems more intimate – describing the dying
  man's experience from the inside. Owen's poem is written in the
  first person, but the dead man is only seen from the outside and
  could represent any or all soldiers. The atmosphere is more cold
  and remote.
- Both extract B and *Futility* begin with hope that with warmth
  and light (*lamps*; *warm blood*; *the sun*) the dead or dying man
  can be *roused*. Both cry out against the waste of life. Sassoon's
  poem suggests death is a release, with soothing images of
  warmth, *Silence and safety*, while the mood of *Futility* remains
  bleak and cold. Sassoon's poem is more purely descriptive and
  the predominant emotion is sadness; Owen's, however, is bitter
  despair at the pointlessness of a life that ends in death on the
  battlefield.

• All three poems are concerned with death and describe some of the saddest aspects of war truthfully and compassionately; and all three include some images and ideas that are beautiful. For example, Sassoon's description of the silence as *Aqueous like floating rays of amber light,/Soaring and quivering in the wings of sleep*, or the ideas of the gentle *touch* of the sun in *Futility*. *I Saw His Round Mouth's Crimson* is perhaps less concerned with compassion and more with presenting a picture of death which is beautiful. The dying man merges with the images of the sunset as the poet watches the life fade out of him: *the magnificent recession of farewell*. Death/night arrives and his eyes become fixed, like *stars lighting*, but these are in the *different skies* of another world. Simultaneously there is the suggestion that the universe is 'indifferent' to his death.

Owen was also inspired by Sassoon's angrier, more satirical poems and immediately began to experiment with this style himself. After meeting Sassoon for the first time, Owen stayed up all night to draft *The Dead-Beat*. However, it has been suggested that Owen later began to question this way of writing, which some critics considered to be more propaganda than poetry (Hibberd, *Wilfred Owen: A New Biography*, pages 335, 369).

Activity

Read Sassoon's poem *They* reproduced below, along with Owen's *The Dead-Beat* (page 29) and *The Chances* (page 39). (If you have access to an anthology, it is worth looking at other poems by Sassoon, such as *Base Details*, *The Hero* or *The General*.)

They

The Bishop tells us: 'When the boys come back
They will not be the same; for they'll have fought
In a just cause: they lead the last attack
On Anti-Christ; their comrades' blood has bought
New right to breed an honourable race,
They have challenged Death and dared him face to face.'

'We're none of us the same!' the boys reply.
'For George lost both his legs; and Bill's stone blind;
Poor Jim's shot through the lungs and like to die;
And Bert's gone syphilitic: you'll not find
A chap who's served that hasn't found *some* change.'
And the Bishop said: 'The ways of God are strange!'

(Sassoon, *The War Poems*, page 57)

What similarities and differences do you notice between these poems?

Discussion

- Real or realistic incidents are the basis of the poems. Owen pointed out on a draft of *The Dead-Beat* that he had used 'the very words!' of the doctor.
- Both poets write in a bitter tone, critical of those in authority who have no empathy for the soldiers and make no effort to understand. The Bishop in *They* spouts the old-fashioned rhetoric of war, while the doctor and officer in *The Dead-Beat* are utterly unsympathetic to the soldier who has collapsed.
- The poems are written from different viewpoints. In *They*, Sassoon narrates the poem from the point of view of 'us' back at home, relating the words of the Bishop and then those of the ordinary soldiers. Owen writes *The Dead-Beat* from the point of view of an officer, impatient with the malingering soldier. He quotes the words of the soldier, a stretcher-bearer and a doctor. The poems draw attention to the difference between the official version of events and the reality that was often hidden from those at home.
- Direct speech and colloquial language are often used. The language of people in authority is differentiated from the vernacular dialect and slang of the soldiers.

All of these literary influences contributed in some way to Owen's style, but it was the way they came together with the very particular subject matter of his war experience and his unique personal response to it, along with his feeling for language, that resulted in his greatest work.

Form and technique

The majority of Owen's poems tend to be **lyrical** in the sense that they explore the writer's reflections about a particular situation, emotion, idea or on an important moment. This does not mean that they cannot also be **narrative** or dramatic. Poems like *Inspection* (page 21), *Dulce et Decorum Est* (page 28) or *The Sentry* (page 47), for example, tell stories of incidents, but they also strongly evoke and express the feelings aroused by the experiences they relate, leaving the reader with the sense of a mood or image rather than a narrative. Welland calls these 'poems of **dramatic description**' as opposed to 'poems of **imaginative description**' (*Wilfred Owen: A Critical Study*, pages 68, 73).

Voices and viewpoints

Owen adopts a range of different **viewpoints** for his imaginative descriptions:

*   In poems like *Anthem for Doomed Youth* (page 22), *The Send-Off* (page 39), and *Spring Offensive* (page 48), he is an impersonal, external presence, describing the scene, often indicating by his choice of words that he empathizes deeply with those involved, but leaving us, as readers, to feel our own responses. In *Disabled* (page 41), he adopts this stance to present an individual character study.
*   In other poems, he writes in the first person, as in *I Saw His Round Mouth's Crimson* (page 24) and *The Show* (page 34), which presents a horrific dream vision.
*   Sometimes Owen indicates that he is involved in the scene, or part of the group, but not individualized, by referring to 'we' or 'us', as in *Insensibility* (page 30) and *Exposure* (page 45).
*   At other times, he expresses his personal beliefs or judgements more directly, as in *Apologia pro Poemate Meo* (page 25) and *Strange Meeting* (page 32).

In the more dramatic poems, he also uses a variety of **narrative voices**:

- In both *Dulce et Decorum Est* (page 28) and *The Sentry* (page 47) he writes as himself, an officer troubled by dreams or recurring memories of particularly horrific incidents – writing at a time when he was a patient at Craiglockhart and reflecting his actual position. Their purpose and mode of address is different, however. While *The Sentry* presents the incident for the reader's open-ended response, *Dulce et Decorum Est* is a direct protest, addressed sarcastically to *My friend*, Jessie Pope, writer of popular jingoistic verses, and others like her.

- In the more satirical or directly critical poems, influenced by Sassoon, he uses a variety of characters, direct speech, colloquial language and slang. For example, in *Inspection* (page 21), which is based on a real incident, he is an officer in dialogue with a soldier and a sergeant, while in *The Chances* (page 39), a soldier relates a conversation with four colleagues. These poems demonstrate Owen's ability to imitate different voices, including working-class speech, without being patronizing.

- *Mental Cases* (page 38) is a more impersonal dialogue based on a biblical source (see Notes on the Poems, page 90) and is more reflective than dramatic.

- *À Terre* (page 43) is a **dramatic monologue**, spoken by one dying soldier to his visitor in hospital but, Owen suggests, representing 'the philosophy of many soldiers' about the prospect of death.

Overall, however, it is a feature of Owen's work that although his poems express a highly personal vision and emotional response, they also have a quality that is impersonal, and this makes them **universally relevant**. He usually avoids the sort of specific references that would tie poems to his own experience. When he describes soldiers waiting tensely for something to happen on the frozen battlefield in *Exposure* or going 'over the top' in *Spring Offensive*, these could be soldiers on either side, at any point in the war, or indeed in any war. In *Strange Meeting*, though, he speaks in the first person, evoking a mythical, mystical dream world which could, again, relate to 'the pity of War' in any time or place.

Poetic forms

Owen also writes in a variety of forms. Initially, following the example of Keats, he wrote sonnets and experimented with traditional rhyming verse forms and blank verse.

The 14-line **sonnet**, with its strict formal structure, is well suited to the lyrical focus on an idea or feeling, but requires discipline from the writer. Owen developed his technical skill by writing many sonnets on set subjects such as *Beauty* and *Happiness* (the latter is reproduced on page 21) for his cousin Leslie Gunston and a friend to criticize. Later, he used the form to reflect on war in *Anthem for Doomed Youth* (page 22).

The **ode** form, very typical of Keats, is a longer reflective poem with a serious tone, often written in praise or celebration of a person or thing, or even of a concept or idea. Owen uses this form in *Insensibility* (page 30).

As his confidence grew, Owen experimented more freely with poetic forms, ranging from short stanzas with regular rhyme and rhythm patterns to almost unstructured verse, with irregular line lengths, shifting stress patterns and the 'incomplete' pararhymes that became his speciality.

Techniques

Pararhyme

Pararhyme is a form of rhyme in which the consonants of the relevant syllable are the same, but the vowels are not. This often involves the consonants both before and after the vowel sounds (e.g. star/stir; escaped/scooped), but may relate only to the final consonants: e.g. once/France.

This technique is considered to be Owen's distinctive contribution to English poetry. In a letter to Sassoon, he calls it his 'Vowel-rime stunt' (Letter 568, *SL*, page 300). It is not quite correct to say that he invented it – other poets had made similar experiments in English and French – but he certainly made it his own, building it into his work until it became an integral part of his style in the great poems he wrote in the last year of his life.

Activity

Look now at *Strange Meeting* on page 32. Read the poem quite slowly, aloud if possible. Otherwise, try to imagine the sounds in your head. Don't worry about understanding every detail. What would you describe as the overall 'feel' of this poem? What did you notice about Owen's poetic technique?

Discussion

How did your experience of reading *Strange Meeting* compare with this account by John Middleton Murry, written in 1921?

I believe that the reader who comes fresh to this poem does not immediately observe the assonant endings. At first he feels only that the blank verse has a mournful, impressive, even oppressive quality of its own; that the poem has a forged unity, a welded and inexorable massiveness. The emotions with which it is charged cannot be escaped; the meaning of the words and the beat of the sounds have the same indivisible message. The tone is single, low, muffled, subterranean. The reader looks again and discovers the technical secret...

(quoted in Hibberd, *Poetry of the First World War*, page 61)

Strange Meeting is probably the most famous – and in some ways obvious – example of Owen's use of pararhyme, in that it is used fairly straightforwardly in couplets throughout the poem. Often, people do respond to pararhyme in the way Murry suggests, with a feeling of discomfort or unease; a sense that something is just not quite right, but we may not be able to identify immediately what that is. If we are used to rhyming poetry, we subconsciously expect to hear 'perfect' or full rhyme, and if we hear instead a pararhyme, we are left subtly unsatisfied. The lines do belong together, but not in such an obvious way. Whereas a full rhyme creates a sense of some-thing being completed, as our expectations are fulfilled – leading us to leave a small pause as we read – pararhymes leave us in expec-tation of something further, leading us always to the next line and creating that sense of 'inexorable' movement onwards through the poem.

It has been suggested that pararhyme provided a way of reflecting the fact that all was not well in the world. The disturbing, disrupted pararhymes were entirely appropriate for writing about the war and 'reflected better than rhyme the disintegration of values in the world around them' (Welland, *Wilfred Owen: A Critical Study*, page 119).

Some critics at the time failed to understand the effect of pararhyme, which presumably seemed very modern to them. Some simply dismissed it as poor technique. Owen was amused when his cousin Leslie Gunston criticized the device: 'Leslie's "musical ear" is offended by my rimes. Isn't that delicious?' (Letter 589, *SL*, page 311).

In other poems, Owen employs pararhyme in varied and less regular ways than he does in *Strange Meeting*. Sometimes he mixes it with full rhyme, as in *Futility* (page 36). Elsewhere it is used to create unpredictable patterns that nevertheless give the poems a subtle sense of cohesion. In *The Show* (page 34), for example, the lines have a fairly regular 5-beat pattern (pentameter), but are arranged in short, unequal stanzas. The use of pararhyme in an unrelated pattern creates links within and between the stanzas. In places, it also draws attention to particular words, reinforcing the horror of the images. For example, at the end of stanza 2, *killed* (9) seems to acquire particular emphasis from its relationship with *uncoiled* two lines earlier.

This draws attention to another point noticed by some critics, which is that Owen almost always chooses the vowel sounds for his pararhymes so that the first has a higher-pitched sound than the second, creating a 'falling' effect, which adds to the sombre feeling of hopelessness in some of his poems. In the opening stanza of *The Show* we have *Death/dearth* and *why/woe*, for example. You may need to read the poems aloud to get the feel of this.

Activity

Look now at the first stanza of *Insensibility* on page 30. If possible, read it aloud.
*   What do you notice about the pattern of pararhymes in these lines?

- Does Owen use the 'falling' pattern here?
- What is the effect of the way pararhymes are used here, do you think?

Discussion

- Pararhyme occurs consecutively in lines 1 and 2 (*killed/cold*), but the uneven line lengths make it less obvious; lines 3 and 4 appear disconnected, but are echoed later, in lines 7 and 10 (*fleers/ flowers*; *feet/fought*); lines 8 and 9 also have consecutive pararhymes (*fooling/filling*). Note the rhyme *brothers/withers* in lines 5 and 6; because the initial consonants differ, these are usually called **half-rhymes.**
- The 'falling' pattern can be detected in *killed/cold, fleers/flowers*; the falling tone on the final *no one bothers* is very clear, and adds to the hopeless feeling that no one cares about what is happening.
- With the unequal line and stanza lengths and lack of an obvious rhythmic stress pattern, the rhymes are quite unobtrusive. At the same time, they wind their way through, binding the poem together in a way that we hear or feel almost subconsciously. The effect is slightly mesmerizing, in a way that is appropriate for the subject matter of the poem – the deadening of sensitivity and feeling that is necessary if soldiers are to survive long periods in the trenches.

Now go on to consider how this is extended throughout the poem. As far as possible, look for connections between the ways rhyme is used and the overall meaning or tone of the poem.

'An exceptionally sensitive ear'

Siegfried Sassoon quickly recognized that Owen's sensitivity to the nuances of language and sound was exceptional.

I have already mentioned the velvety quality of his voice, which suggested the Keatsian richness of his artistry with words. It wasn't a vibrating voice. It had the fluid texture of soft consonants and murmurous music. Hearing him read poetry aloud in his modest unemphatic way, one realized at once that he had an exceptionally sensitive ear. One of his poems begins 'All sounds have been as music to my listening', and his sense of colour was correspondingly absorbent. Sounds and colours, in his verse, were mulled and modulated to a subtle magnificence of sensuous harmonies, and this was noticeable even in his everyday speaking... It can be observed that his work is prevalently deliberate in movement. Stately and processional, it has the rhythm of emotional depth and directness and the verbal resonance of one who felt in glowing primary colours and wrote with solemn melodies in his mind.

(Sassoon, *Siegfried's Journey, 1916–20*, page 62)

You will notice that Sassoon compares Owen's ability to create textures and patterns from words to that of a musician. Pararhyme is only one of the ways he draws on the sound qualities of language to create vivid pictures and images. In descriptive poems he also weaves other kinds of **aural imagery** into his work, using alliteration, assonance, internal rhyme, onomatopoeia, or punctuation that creates long drawn-out lines or short phrases, to create many different effects.

- **Alliteration**
  In *Anthem for Doomed Youth* the sounds of the battlefield are echoed by the repeated hard consonants in

  > Only the stuttering rifles' rapid rattle
  > Can patter out their hasty orisons.

  (3–4)

- **Assonance**
  In *The Send-Off*:

  > Down the close darkening lanes they sang their way
  > To the siding-shed,
  > And lined the train with faces grimly gay.

  (1–3)

  The pattern of repeated sounds adds to the mournful and slightly sinister atmosphere of this scene.

In these lines from *Mental Cases* (page 38), alliteration and assonance are used together to build the sense of horror at what the traumatized soldiers have experienced:

> Wading sloughs of flesh these helpless wander,
> Treading blood from lungs that had loved laughter.
>
> (13–14)

This time soft, hissing consonants, like 's' and 'f', combine with the liquid 'l' to mimic the queasy-making squelch the men experienced as they literally trampled the corpses of their dead companions. Though not spelled uniformly, the vowel sounds of *flesh/helpless* and *blood/lungs/loved* followed by the slightly altered *laughter* intensify this effect.

- **Internal rhyme**
  This is similar to assonance. In the same poem: *Batter of guns and shatter of flying muscles* (16).

- **Onomatopoeia**
  In *The Sentry* (page 47), down-to-earth, graphic words are used to describe how the injured sentry falls into the dugout as a shell explodes in the doorway:

> And thud! flump! thud! down the steep steps came thumping
> And sploshing in the flood, deluging muck,
> The sentry's body
>
> (13–15)

Notice, too, that once again other sound effects, including alliteration and assonance are combined here.

- **Punctuation**
  In *The Show* (page 34) this long sentence, with its string of short clauses separated by commas, builds up in a menacing way that mirrors the massing of troops on the battlefield:

> On dithering feet upgathered, more and more,
> Brown strings, towards strings of grey, with bristling spines,
> All migrants from green fields, intent on mire.
>
> (16–18)

In *Spring Offensive* (page 48), when the men go 'over the top', the word *Exposed* (29) is given a sudden emphasis, by isolating it at the beginning of a new line and following it with a full stop. The word itself is 'exposed' in a way that mirrors the vulnerability of the men. This creates a split second of tension, before they are 'instantly' engulfed by enemy fire.

You will have seen from these examples that it is rather artificial to try to separate these technical devices in Owen's work. Really, it is the way they all work together that creates the powerful effects in his poems, and it is likely that he often chose his words quite intuitively, relying on his 'sensitive ear' to guide him. Responding to criticism from his cousin, Owen described his technique as 'doing in poetry what the advanced composers are doing in music' (Letter 589, *SL*, page 311).

Activity

One poem in which aural imagery is used with particular intensity is *Exposure* (page 45).

Look now at the first stanza of the poem:

Our brains ache, in the merciless iced east winds that knive us...
Wearied we keep awake because the night is silent...
Low, drooping flares confuse our memory of the salient...
Worried by silence, sentries whisper, curious, nervous,
        But nothing happens.

If possible, find a copy of the poem you can annotate. Mark or note all the ways you can find in which Owen has chosen his words for their qualities of sound. What is the effect of this stanza on the reader?

Discussion

- Our attention may be caught immediately by the assonance of *brains ache*, and later of *iced* and *knive* which, along with the alliteration of *merciless iced east wind*, with its repeated hissed 's' sounds, gives a menacing feel to the description of the deadly, freezing wind.
- The phrase *knive us* is echoed with a pararhyme, but not until

line 4. As usual, the pararhyme, *nervous*, has a lower pitched sound than *knive us*, giving the 'falling' effect that contributes to the sense of hopelessness and inertia that pervades this poem.

- The 'falling' effect also occurs with the pararhyme of *silent* and *salient*.
- In line 2, there is alliteration in *Wearied we keep awake*, where the slow 'w' sound increases the feeling of exhaustion, and more assonance in *night is silent*, which again echoes *iced* and *knive* in line 1.
- The pattern of soft consonant and vowel sounds in line 3, *Low drooping flares confuse*, continues the slightly hypnotic effect of the stanza.
- In line 4, *Worried* echoes *wearied* in line 2; *silence* again echoes lines 1 and 2; the repetition of 's' sounds and the succession of words separated by commas mimics the anxious, sporadic whispering of the sentries and builds the tension.
- The final short line, *But nothing happens*, is anti-climactic and might be expected to break the tension, but instead, for some reason, it seems to hold or *sustain* the tension, so that in stanza 2 it continues to intensify.

However, it is the overall effect that is important. Owen has woven language into complex, interdependent patterns that build up an impression of the deadly cold that numbs the men's minds and a sinister sense of the experience of waiting, apparently endlessly, in a state of heightened tension.

Imagery, colour and the senses

Along with Owen's sensitivity to the sounds of language, Sassoon also pointed out his rich sense of colour, suggesting that this reflected the fact that his emotional responses were strong and pure – he 'felt in glowing primary colours' (*Siegfried's Journey, 1916–20*, page 62). There is perhaps more variety of colour to be found in his non-war poetry. The colours of the war are dark, or diminished, often *grey*, like the threatening clouds in *Exposure*, but which are also German uniforms, or the *ghastly* suit of the soldier in *Disabled*. Against this background, flashes of bright colour stand out vividly, such as the gold of the buttercups in *Spring Offensive* (14–15). Above all, the colours of blood are given particular attention. It is *all things red* in *Insensibility*, and the red *stained stones* in *Greater Love*, where it is linked with romantic *Red lips* and decadent images of torn, bleeding mouths; elsewhere, it is 'scarlet', 'crimson', or 'purple'; in *Mental Cases*, the men who have seen too much blood see its colours in everything: *Sunlight seems a blood-smear; night comes blood-black* (21).

Owen's visual sense also manifests in his powerful use of **simile** and **metaphor**.

Activity

Look now at *Dulce et Decorum Est* (page 28). Note examples of simile in the poem. Discuss the effect of these.

Discussion

- In the opening lines, two similes compare the retreating soldiers to *old beggars under sacks* and coughing *hags*, so that these young men appear ancient, sick and decrepit.
- The soldier who fails to fit his gas mask quickly enough is *flound'ring like a man in fire or lime* (12), which conveys both that he appears to be drowning and that he is writhing in anguish as if in contact with flames or a caustic substance.
- Seen through the visor of the narrator's gas mask, the dying man appears to be deep underwater, *As under a green sea* (14), giving a nightmarish, unreal quality to the image and perhaps also the suggestion of slow motion.
- In the final stanza, a series of similes combine to make the image of the gas victim as disturbing and horrific as possible. His face is *hanging* and *like a devil's sick of sin*: things must be extreme for the devil to tire of sin. The vision of the sick man's symptoms is *Obscene as cancer*, the most terrifying of diseases, while *bitter as the cud/Of vile, incurable sores on innocent tongues* suggests the man almost chewing at his burned mouth and tongue and the *sores* may be those of syphilis, a disease that is as inappropriate as possible for an *innocent* boy.

Owen's imagery does not appeal only to the aural and visual senses, though. In many poems all the senses are invoked, giving the reader a multi-dimensional impression of what is described.

Activity

In *The Show* on page 34, Owen creates an extended metaphorical dream image of the battlefield seen from above. (See Notes on the Poems, pages 85–6 for more about the origins of this 'vision'.)

- Read *The Show* once, straight through. What would you describe as the 'feel' of this poem?
- Now discuss or make notes on the ways Owen has used metaphor and the senses here, considering how these contribute to the poem's effect.

Discussion

- Possible initial responses to this poem might be a feeling of distaste or disgust, of menace, or foreboding.
- The extended metaphor Owen uses here is a bird's-eye view of a sinister, diseased, fantasy landscape, *cratered like the moon with hollow woe* (4), in which strange creatures, which appear like worms or caterpillars, attack and devour each other. The colours, textures and smell of the landscape are all included. Its details are described as signs of disease, but contain clues that the real subject is the battlefield, such as the *beard* (6), that is actually the tangle of barbed wire that guarded the trenches. The land is *weak with sweats of dearth* (3), like the swamped, poisoned fields of the Somme which were *pitted* with the *pocks and scabs* (5) of thousands of shell-holes and craters.

  From above, the trenches form apparently meaningless *slimy paths* (10), in which dugouts are the foul-smelling *hidden holes* (13) of the unpleasant creatures, which avoid daylight.

  The *caterpillars* (7) are platoons of men, *brown strings* of British troops in khaki, and *grey* Germans, with the *bristling spines* (17) of their spiked helmets. In the final stanza, one of these *worms* seems to be Owen's own platoon, which has had its head bitten off. He, as their *head*, has become separated from his men.

  Words like *bristling* and *slimy* draw on the sense of touch, as does the idea that the creatures *spawn*, while a kinaesthetic (bodily feeling) response is evoked by the description of the way the creatures *curve, loop, and straighten... curl, lift, and flatten* as they writhe with the *agonies* of their *bitten backs* (21–2).

For most of the poem sound is absent. Distanced by the *vague height* (1) the landscape is eerily silent. The only sound is the *deepening moan* of Death (25), as the narrator falls back to earth.

Senses and metaphor combine to build a powerful, disturbing image that affects the reader on more than one level.

Critical reception

Only four of Owen's poems were published in his lifetime and none of these was a major work. He was a 'poet's poet', his talent recognized by his peers, but too far ahead of general opinion to have gained a mainstream audience during the war. He was delighted by his friendship with Sassoon and gratified to have the support of Harold Monro and other writers in his circle. In December 1917, he received an encouraging letter from Robert Graves: 'Don't make any mistake, Owen, you are a damned fine poet already & will be more so... Puff out your chest a little, Owen, & be big, for you've more right than most of us...' (quoted in Hibberd, *Wilfred Owen: A New Biography*, 2002, page 368).

Not long after, though, Graves was more critical. He disapproved of writing poetry that was too much like propaganda: 'For God's sake cheer up and write more optimistically... a poet should have a spirit above wars' (quoted in Hibberd, page 369).

For Owen's response to this, see *Apologia pro Poemate Meo* (page 25 and the notes on page 75). The debate about whether or not his concern with making a protest detracts from his poetry is a recurring theme in criticism of his work. Some critics suggest this made his work too personal, whereas others are convinced that his ability to make it universal is one of his strongest qualities.

Siegfried Sassoon published the first edition of Owen's poems in 1920 and it was well received. Introducing the volume, Sassoon wrote (page v):

> He never wrote his poems (as so many war-poets did) to make the effect of a personal gesture. He pitied others; he did not pity himself. In the last year of his life he attained a clear vision of what he needed to say, and these poems survive him as his true and splendid testament.
>
> (quoted in Hibberd, *Poetry of the First World War*, page 53)

Edmund Blunden, writing soon afterwards in an article in *The Athenaeum* ('The Real War', 10 December 1920, page 807), endorsed Owen's skill with language:

> Owen was one of the few spokesmen of the ordinary fighting man... 1917 heard for the first time the articulate voice of rebellion; it was high time.
>
> [...]
>
> In Owen we lost a poet of rare force. We have hinted at the spirit of his verse; the letter is as masterly. The very make of his language is hard and remorseless or strange and sombre as he wills; the discovery of final assonances in place of rhyme may mark a new age in poetry.
>
> (quoted in Hibberd, *Poetry of the First World War*, page 55)

while John Middleton Murry praises his emotional power:

> 'The Poetry is in the pity.' Whatever the new generation of poets may think or say, Owen had the secret in those words. The source of all enduring poetry lies in an intense and overwhelming emotion. The emotion must be overwhelming, and suffered as it were to the last limit of the soul's capacity.
>
> (quoted in Hibberd, *Poetry of the First World War*, page 60)

The patriotic poet Sir Henry Newbolt, writing in a letter dated 2 August 1924, was less enthusiastic:

> Owen and the rest of the broken men rail at the Old Men who sent the young to die: they have suffered cruelly, but in the nerves and not the heart – they haven't the experience to know

the extreme human agony... I don't think these shell-shocked war poems will move our grandchildren greatly.

(quoted in Hibberd, *Poetry of the First World War*, page 65)

In 1936, however, W.B. Yeats, editing *The Oxford Book of Modern Verse*, omitted Owen's work altogether. There was an outcry: Owen's work was by now more widely known and admired. Here Yeats defends his decision in a scathing letter dated 21 December 1936:

My Anthology continues to sell & the critics get more & more angry. When I excluded Wilfred Owen, whom I consider unworthy of the poets' corner of a country newspaper, I did not know I was excluding a revered sandwich-board Man of the revolution & that some body has put his worst & most famous poem in a glass-case in the British Museum – however if I had known it I would have excluded him just the same. He is all blood, dirt & sucked sugar-stick (Look at the selection in Faber's Anthology – he calls poets 'bards', a girl a 'maid' & talks about 'Titanic wars'). There is every excuse for him but none for those who like him.

(quoted in Hibberd, *Poetry of the First World War*, page 80)

When we read what critics have to say, especially those writing more recently, we need to be aware that they may have a political viewpoint or belong to a particular school of literary criticism which colours how they view writers and their work. Owen's work has been seen through various lenses and used to endorse ideologies such as socialism and feminism. During the 1930s, for example:

Owen had his impact on the younger English poets, notably Auden, Spender, MacNeice and Day Lewis. Leftist or Communist in sympathy at that time, they were attracted to his use of poetry for a political purpose, his idealisation and celebration of common men, and his wrathful indignation against those who were exploiting them.

(quoted in Hibberd, *Poetry of the First World War*, page 166)

More recently, feminist critics have suggested that his work is an indictment of patriarchal culture in which 'male shall dominate female, and elder male shall dominate younger':

> Owen, in his 'Parable', rather than postulating an 'ideal'
> authoritarian figure in the myth of Abraham, is showing us how
> any authoritarian patriarch is likely to become corrupted by
> power as well as by pride.
>
> (Jennifer Breen, ed., *Wilfred Owen: Selected Poetry and Prose*,
> pages 175–6)

Dominic Hibberd and others have also sought to bring the possible homosexual element in Owen's work out of the shadows.

Not surprisingly, perhaps, war poetry like Owen's was less popular during the Second World War and the period of austerity that followed. However, during the 1960s, Owen's work began to reach a wider audience. Dennis Welland wrote the first substantial critique of his poems and the composer Benjamin Britten used a selection of them in the impressive *War Requiem*, written for the dedication of the new Coventry Cathedral in 1962.

Anti-war feeling ran high during the American war in Vietnam and there was widespread fear of nuclear attack as the Cold War intensified through the 1970s and 1980s. Wilfred Owen, now a household name, was quoted by peace campaigners and studied in schools. Fascination with the First World War and its writers continues to show no sign of abating.

Essay Questions

1   The poet Robert Graves's advice to Owen was: 'For God's sake cheer up and write more optimistically... a poet should have a spirit above wars.' How far would you agree with his view that Owen's poetry is too pessimistic?

2   Discuss the ways in which Owen presents death in his poems. Either analyse three poems in detail or range more widely through his work.

3   *Dulce et Decorum Est* (page 28) and *Apologia pro Poemate Meo* (page 25) are both poems in which Owen has a message to convey. Compare and contrast the ways in which he makes his point in each poem.

4   W.B. Yeats complained that Owen's work was 'all blood, dirt & sucked sugar-stick'. What do you think he meant? Do you agree with his view?

5   How does Owen use language to create his effects in *Exposure* (page 45)?

6   Compare the ways in which Owen presents the survivors of war in *Disabled* (page 41) and *Mental Cases* (page 38).

7   The critic Philip Hobsbaum suggests that it is 'too simple to regard Owen as the poet who hated war'. How far would you agree with this view?

8   In 1924 Sir Henry Newbolt described Wilfred Owen's poetry as 'limited, almost all on one note'. Do you think this is a fair assessment of Owen's poetry?

9   'In these poems there is no more rebellion, but only pity and regret...'. Do you agree with this comment by John Middleton Murry?

10 In 1936, W.B. Yeats refused to include Owen's work in *The Oxford Book of English Verse*, saying that 'passive suffering is

not a theme for poetry'. Imagine that you are compiling a new anthology of British poetry. Argue a case **either** for **or** against including poems by Wilfred Owen in the selection.

If you argue 'for', name the poems you would select and why. In your discussion, focus on three or four poems in detail, or range more widely through his work.

11 'I don't think these shell-shocked war poems will move our grandchildren greatly,' said the patriotic poet Sir Henry Newbolt. To what extent do you find Owen's poems moving? Refer either to three poems in detail or to a wider selection in your discussion.

12 Explore the ways in which Owen presents his ideas and creates his effects in *The Show* (page 34).

13 It has been suggested that Owen wrote his letters to his mother not just for her to read, but for 'posterity'. What evidence of this can you find?

14 Compare the style of writing in Letters 330 (page 51) and 673 (page 64).

15 Compare the ways Owen describes his experiences in Letter 480 (page 54) and *The Sentry* (page 47).

Chronology

Date	Events in Wilfred Owen's life	Historical/political/war events
1893	Born at Oswestry, Shropshire, son of Tom Owen, a railway clerk, and Susan (née Shaw)	
1895	Mary Owen born	
1897	Harold Owen born	Queen Victoria's Diamond Jubilee
1898		Zeppelin builds the first airship
1899–1902		The Boer War
1900	The Owen family move to Birkenhead, on Merseyside Colin Owen born Wilfred begins studying at the Birkenhead Institute	
1901		Queen Victoria dies and is succeeded by her son Edward VII
1903		First aeroplane flight
1907	The Owens move to Shrewsbury when Tom is promoted to a senior position on the railway Wilfred attends Shrewsbury Technical School and goes on to become a Pupil-Teacher (trainee primary-school teacher)	

1910		Edward VII dies; George V becomes King
1911		
April	Owen discovers the work of John Keats and begins training himself to write poetry	
October	He goes to the village of Dunsden, Oxfordshire, as Parish Assistant to the Revd Henry Wigan	
1912	Owen becomes a part-time external student at University College, Reading, studying botany and, later, English	Sinking of the *Titanic*
	He begins to find the evangelical Christianity and heavy routine at Dunsden stifling and deadening	
1913		
January	Owen has a crisis of faith and leaves Dunsden, returning to Shrewsbury, where he is ill for several weeks	
May	He sits the entrance exams for Reading University, but fails to win a scholarship	
September	Moves to Bordeaux, France, to teach English at the Berlitz language school	

1914		
July	Leaves the Berlitz school to become private tutor to Mme Léger and her family, staying in a villa at Bagnères-de-Bigorre in the Pyrenees	During July, the Germans invade Belgium and attack the Russians in Galicia
August	Owen meets the French poet Laurent Tailhade, who becomes a friend and mentor	On 4 August, war is declared in France and the French government moves to Bordeaux
September	Owen returns to Bordeaux and works as a freelance teacher of English	In Britain, recruiting campaigns begin
November		Trench warfare begins on the Western Front
December	Owen accepts a post as tutor to the sons of the de la Touche family, and moves to join them at Mérignac, near Bordeaux	The first mines are exploded
1915		
January	Remains at Mérignac as the Channel is considered unsafe for travel	War in Turkey begins; the Dardanelles Campaign and the landings at Gallipoli
April		Gas is first used, at Ypres
		Italy joins the war
		Russians suffer heavy defeat, losing one million soldiers

May	Visits London and Shrewsbury	In Britain, the Coalition Government takes over from the Liberals
	Returns to Bordeaux	German submarine campaign in the Atlantic; the liner *Lusitania* is sunk
June	Owen considers joining the Artists' Rifles	Zeppelin raids on England begin
July–September	Travels to London, then home to Shrewsbury	British and French Offensive on the Western Front makes little headway
October	Joins the Artists' Rifles and finds lodgings in London	
November	Meets Harold Monro at The Poetry Bookshop in London	Stalemate continues on the Western Front
	Becomes a Cadet with the Artists' Rifles at Hare Hall Camp, Essex	
1916 February	On a training course in London before transferring to Officers' School	Conscription introduced in Britain
		Allied troops are evacuated from Gallipoli
		Battle of Verdun
March	Stays in lodgings at The Poetry Bookshop; shows Monro his poems	

April		British troops in Turkey forced to surrender
June	Commissioned into the Manchester Regiment and joins the 5th (Reserve) Battalion at Milford Camp, Surrey	
July		Battle of the Somme begins
Sept.– November	Various placements; training in musketry	The Russians lose another million men First use of tanks
December	After Christmas leave, travels to Base Camp, Etaples, France	Lloyd George becomes Prime Minister
1917 January	Joins 2nd Manchester Regiment near Beaumont Hamel on the Somme. Goes twice into the Front Line, the second time in severe cold weather	Submarine warfare a growing threat; ships sail in convoys for protection
February	Transport course at Abbeville	Food shortages in Britain; bread and other foods are rationed
March	Rejoins the battalion; suffers concussion falling into a cellar and spends some days at a Casualty Clearing Station	
April	Back in action at Savy Wood	French offensive fails

May	Evacuated to Casualty Clearing Station with shell-shock	Mutiny in French army
June	Owen in hospitals in France and Wales before entering Craiglockhart War Hospital, near Edinburgh	
July	Becomes editor of the hospital magazine, *The Hydra* Siegfried Sassoon arrives	British offensive – Third Battle of Ypres (Passchendaele) – no progress; terrible conditions in trenches continue
August	Introduces himself to Sassoon	
September	Drafts several important poems Growing friendship with Sassoon	
October	Medical board declares Owen fit for light duties	Bolshevik revolution in Russia
November	Meets Robert Ross, Arnold Bennett and H.G. Wells Joins 5th Manchester Regiment at Scarborough; in charge of domestic arrangements at the Officers' Mess	British victory at Cambrai and small advance
December	Sassoon returns to France	Russia pulls out of the war

1918		
January	'Miners' is published in the magazine *The Nation*	
February		Women over 30 are given the vote
March	Moves to Northern Command Depot, Ripon, Yorkshire; rents a room in a nearby cottage to use as a study, and works hard on poetry	Treaty of Brest-Litovsk forces Russians to give up huge amounts of land in the Ukraine, Finland and the Baltic states Germans begin huge 'Spring Offensive' and advance towards Paris
May		French and American troops stop the German advance
June	Now graded fit for general service, Owen rejoins the regiment at Scarborough Two poems published in *The Nation*	
July	Sassoon returns home wounded	Allied counter-offensive begins Germans now in retreat Disintegration of the Austro-Hungarian Empire

August	Owen visits Sassoon in hospital before travelling once more to France	Allies on the offensive; Battles of the Marne and Amiens; the Germans are forced to retreat towards the border
September	At Amiens with 2nd Manchesters	
October	Owen awarded Military Cross for his part in successful action on the Beaurevoir-Fonsomme Line Back into the Line to prepare for an attack on the Sambre–Oise Canal, near Ors	
November	Shot and killed while helping his men in the crossing of the Sambre–Oise Canal	The war ends with the signing of the Armistice at 11 a.m. on 11th November

Further Reading

Editions of Wilfred Owen's poems and letters

The standard edition of the poems is:

Jon Stallworthy (ed.) *Wilfred Owen: The Complete Poems and Fragments*, 2 vols. (Oxford University Press in conjunction with Chatto & Windus, 1983)

A representative selection of the poems is available in paperback in:

Jon Stallworthy (ed.) *Wilfred Owen: The War Poems* (Chatto & Windus, 1994)

The letters are published in:

Harold Owen and John Bell (eds) *Wilfred Owen: Collected Letters* (Oxford University Press, 1967)

A paperback selection in which many of the letters are reproduced is:

John Bell (ed.) *Wilfred Owen: Selected Letters* (Oxford University Press, 1985; 2nd edn 1998) (referred to in this edition as *SL*)

Biography

Dominic Hibberd, *Wilfred Owen: A New Biography* (Weidenfeld & Nicolson, 2002; paperback edn Phoenix, 2003)

Jon Stallworthy, *Wilfred Owen: A Biography* (Oxford University Press and Chatto & Windus, 1974)

Critical books

Dominic Hibberd, *Owen the Poet* (Macmillan, 1986)

Dominic Hibberd (ed.) *Poetry of the First World War: A Selection of Critical Essays* (Macmillan Press, 1981)

Douglas Kerr, *Wilfred Owen's Voices* (Oxford University Press, 1993)

Dennis S.R. Welland, *Wilfred Owen: A Critical Study* (Chatto & Windus, 1960)

Background reading

Pat Barker, *The Regeneration Trilogy: Regeneration; The Eye in the Door; The Ghost Road* (Viking Press, 1991, 1993 and 1995)

Santanu Das, *Touch and Intimacy in First World War Literature* (Cambridge University Press, 2005)

Sebastian Faulks, *Birdsong* (Hutchinson, 1993)

Paul Fussell, *The Great War and Modern Memory* (Oxford University Press, 1975)

Brian Gardner, *Up the Line to Death: The War Poets 1914–1918* (Methuen, 1964; rev. edn 1976)

Susan Hill, *Strange Meeting* (Hamish Hamilton, 1971)

Stephen Macdonald, *Not About Heroes: The Friendship of Siegfried Sassoon and Wilfred Owen* (Faber, 1983)

Harold Owen, *Journey from Obscurity* (Oxford University Press, 1988)

Catherine Reilly (ed.) *Scars upon My Heart: Women's Poetry and Verse of the First World War* (Virago, 1981)

Siegfried Sassoon, *The Complete Memoirs of George Sherston* (Faber, 1937)

Siegfried Sassoon, *Siegfried's Journey, 1916–20* (Faber, 1945)

Siegfried Sassoon, *The War Poems* (Faber, 1983)

Jon Stallworthy, *Anthem for Doomed Youth* (Constable & Robinson, 2005)

Jon Stallworthy (ed.) *The Oxford Book of War Poetry* (Oxford University Press, 1984)

A.J.P. Taylor, *The First World War* (Hamish Hamilton, 1963)

Deborah West (ed.) *John Keats: Selected Poems* (Oxford Student Texts, Oxford University Press, 2006)

Merryn Williams, *Wilfred Owen* (Border Lines series, Bridgend, Seren Books, 1993)

Websites

www.hcu.ox.ac.uk/jtap/warpoems.htm
This site provides the texts of Owen's poems together with facsimiles of many of his working manuscripts, which give insights into how he worked on his poems.

www.bbc.co.uk/history/worldwars/wwone/
Full of useful background information about the First World War, with plenty of illustrations.

www.nationalarchives.gov.uk/pathways/firstworldwar/
Includes a broad selection of documents, audio and video material about the First World War.